THE PLOT WHISPERER

Secrets of Story Structure
Any Writer Can Master

MARTHA ALDERSON, *Founder of PlotWriMo*

Adams Media
New York London Toronto Sydney New Delhi

Adams Media
An Imprint of Simon & Schuster, Inc.
57 Littlefield Street
Avon, Massachusetts 02322

For information about special discounts for bulk purchases, please contact Simon
& Schuster Special Sales at 1-866-506-1949 or business@simonandschuster.com.

The Simon & Schuster Speakers Bureau can bring authors to your live event. For
more information or to book an event contact the Simon & Schuster Speakers
Bureau at 1-866-248-3049 or visit our website at www.simonspeakers.com.

Manufactured in the United States of America

20 19 18 17 16 15 14 13

Library of Congress Cataloging-in-Publication Data has been applied for.

ISBN 978-1-4405-2588-9
ISBN 978-1-4405-2847-7 (ebook)

Dedication

To my mother Gertrud Inga Maria Svensson Stockton
For encouraging my imagination and always inspiring me

Acknowledgments

For your enthusiastic belief in me, Jill Corcoran, I thank you. To Ronnie Herman, thank you for your expertise. To everyone at Adams Media and especially Paula Munier for your vision for this book and, for your tireless help and coaxing, Peter Archer, I am forever grateful.

I would not be the Plot Whisperer if not for all my writing buddies, especially Luisa Adams and Teresa LeYung Ryan, and everyone who showed up for my plot workshops and retreats and requested plot consultations from all over the world, and for all the writers who blogged and Tweeted and Facebooked about my work, and commented on my blog and YouTube channel, as well as everyone who extended me a forum in which to teach plot. A special thanks goes out to the University of California Santa Cruz for inviting me to teach plot through its extension program.

I have learned from every writer I have ever met and I could not have written this book without you. Thank you.

To my husband, Bobby Ray Alderson, for his endless patience and belief in me, I love you now and forever.

A special thanks to Luisa Adams for sharing her passion about the two sides of the brain and her visceral aversion to all things plot, except for me.

And lastly, thank you Rosie, Milo, Mara, Jodie, and George for pulling aside the veil and revealing to me the other side . . .

CONTENTS

CONTENTS

INTRODUCTION
THE PLOT WHISPERER

It takes a lot of energy and a lot of neurosis to write a novel. If you were really sensible, you'd do something else.

—Laurence Durrell

Something urges you to pick up this book. A story in your imagination will not let you go. The characters are speaking to you, and they're demanding answers, asking you what to do with them. Perhaps a scene haunts your dreams. Interweaving themes run through your mind, vibrating with excitement. You feel an uncontrollable compulsion to get the story down on paper.

So far, so good. But now you want to know where to begin a story and how get off to a good start. Slowly it becomes clear to you that you're held back by fear—fear of a painful trial that will expose your inner self to others.

Maybe you already write, have been published multiple times, and understand writing is more complicated than simply putting words on a page. Still, plot bewilders you. You are eager—perhaps, desperate—to unlock the mystery of good story structure. You ask: How do I create a memorable novel, memoir, or screenplay? You want a more fulfilling relationship with your story and your writing life.

If I've just described you, then you have come to the right place.

My name is Martha Alderson. I am the Plot Whisperer.

My intention in writing this book is to share the insights I have gained about plot and character, structure and form, thanks to years of teaching and consulting with writers from five years old to 102. I conduct plot workshops for writers of all genres who are intent on creating a worthy project. In one-on-one plot consultations, I listen to writers from all over the world recount scenes and visions for their stories. Throughout the process, I suggest plot parameters, offer tips on theme and character, and recommend tricks for layering and pacing.

The more writers I interact with, the more keenly I feel the universality and interconnectedness of our shared journeys through life together, especially those of us stubborn enough to pluck words from our imaginations and offer them to the world.

Anyone who wants to write or is in the process of writing a novel, short story, memoir, or screenplay faces the daunting task of creating several plots and multiple scenes. This book will guide you through the process of writing the story inside of you. Along the way I include Plot Whisper tips and exercises to improve your plotting skills, and The Writer's Way advice about how to expand your writing life.

The plot help in this book is rooted in my long experience and knowledge of the inner workings of real and imagined stories. I give all-day plot workshops to writers of children's books through the Society of Children's Book Writers and Illustrators and at children's shelters to children and teens taken from their homes into protective custody. With them I examine picture books, middle grade, and young adult fiction. I attend Romance Writers of America chapter meetings where I plot out love stories in all subgenres of romance novels. I help authors craft cunning murders in mystery novels; and I assist memoirists connected with the National Association of Memoir Writers. At the Writers Store in Los Angeles, I help script and screenwriters plot movies, television sitcoms, and docudramas.

I have had the honor of working with multipublished, award-winning, and bestselling novelists across all genres. I have even addressed a conference of 500 corporate defense lawyers interested in using plot to create more compelling case presentations and keep the jury engaged.

The Universal Story

My most important insight is this: All of us face antagonists and hurdles, hopes and joys, and by meeting these challenges we can transform our lives. I have come to believe that every scene in every book is part of a Universal Story that flows throughout our lives, both in our imaginations and in the reality that surrounds us.

Every story ever told participates in this universal pattern as words grow and expand into sentences, paragraphs, and chapters. What is left after the end of the story has the potential to transform not only the writer but all those who read the story as well.

I teach the Universal Story to writers through plot. Though difficult to accomplish successfully, plot is critical to stories. As I continue to teach and write and consult, I gain new insights into plot . . . and into writers' lives.

The transformative qualities of plot and the concept of a Universal Story were with me even at the beginning of my writing life, though I could barely recognize them. First, I had to learn how to pull aside the veil between the seen and the unseen worlds. Before you roll your eyes, take a deep breath and bear with me.

I have had a lifelong desire to understand energy. I saw that successful people whom I admired were filled with energy, and I searched for ways to activate that power in myself. In the 1990s I sold my learning clinic for children and started writing fiction. At the same time, I was faced with a personal crisis: a series of dogs with whom I was hopelessly in love required extensive medical intervention. Eager to support their healing, I visited an alternative veterinarian. She taught me how to channel and use energy to heal others. That is when I first learned of the veil and what is on the other side.

I separated my life into daily writing sessions and energy work with my dogs. Later, my writing life focused on teaching plotting techniques. My energy work moved from my dogs to cancer patients, hospital-bound children, people facing death, family, friends, my husband, and me.

Slowly, I became aware that the flow of energy I feel in healing also moves in my writing. It penetrates the stories I analyze and the lives of the writers with whom I work; it embraces the lives of those I love, and it permeates all nature.

In this book, I share with you the Universal Story: where to spot it and how to use it to create better stories and a better life. Natural-born storytellers tap into the Universal Story intuitively. Others must learn how to use the Universal Story to write compelling stories of their own.

Throughout this book I've included plot planners and scene trackers to show the overall plot of a story and how every element in it works in each scene to advance the story.

My goal is for you to feel more strongly the link between the transformative energy in stories and the possibilities available to you in your own life. I want to open up a new dimension of life you never before imagined. Thus, this book can be of benefit to artists and creative people of all types.

You bring to your writing, your art, and your stories a piece of yourself. In return, the act of creating gives you the possibility of something even greater: true transformation.

I hope you come away from this book with practical techniques to integrate the energy of the Universal Story into your story. After using these ideas, you'll begin to understand yourself better. You'll see your writing in a different light. The ways you interact with your writing and with the world around you will shift.

Be forewarned, though. Writing a story can expand your everyday life; it can also destroy the person you are now. I ask you to commit to your own journey as your protagonist embarks on hers. Explore your true essence. Whether you emerge from the experience better or worse is your choice. But I believe the act of writing offers you the possibility of transformation.

You imagine yourself into being a writer. Your imagination allows you to see worlds invisible to others. Imagine the Universal Story into reality and reclaim a miraculous and mysterious way of being.

Figure 1. The Plot Planner: Above and Below

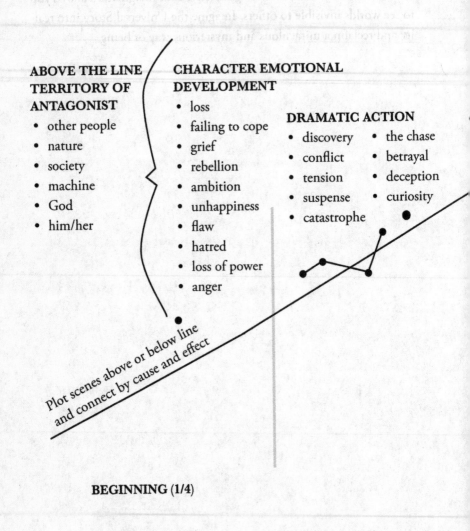

ABOVE THE LINE TERRITORY OF ANTAGONIST
- other people
- nature
- society
- machine
- God
- him/her

CHARACTER EMOTIONAL DEVELOPMENT
- loss
- failing to cope
- grief
- rebellion
- ambition
- unhappiness
- flaw
- hatred
- loss of power
- anger

DRAMATIC ACTION
- discovery
- conflict
- tension
- suspense
- catastrophe
- the chase
- betrayal
- deception
- curiosity

Plot scenes above or below line and connect by cause and effect

BEGINNING (1/4)

THEMATIC SIGNIFICANCE
- mood
- metaphor
- sensory details
- setting
- define
- development
- mention

DRAMATIC ACTION
- lull in conflict
- giving info
- telling

**CHARACTER EMOTIONAL
DEVELOPMENT**
- calm
- coping
- planning
- solving problems
- contemplative
- in control

**BELOW THE LINE:
TERRITORY OF
PROTAGONIST**

MIDDLE (1/2)

END (1/4)

Figure 2. Scene Tracker Template
Copyright © 2004, Martha Alderson

SCENE TRACKER

Project Name:

Date:

Draft:

Chapter:

Scene/ Summary	Dates/Setting	Character Emotional Development	Goal
SCENE #1			
SCENE #2			
SCENE #3			
OPTIONAL			
OPTIONAL			

Notes:

Dramatic/ Action Plot	Conflict	Emotional Change	Thematic Significance/ Details

CHAPTER ONE
SITTING DOWN TO WRITE

Language is the light of the mind.

—John Stuart Mill

Why is writing important? Because it teaches you about yourself, expands your horizons, and challenges you to discover new truths.

Whether you're writing a novel, memoir, or screenplay, you are writing about a character transformed through the Universal Story. That character pursues a goal. She faces a series of conflicts and obstacles, and as a result, her choices change over time. In the end, she is transformed, and her ultimate transformation creates her anew with a different understanding of herself and her existence.

As you write, you will begin to see a similar pattern emerge in your own life as you face conflicts that arise from your writing. In the end, you, too, will be transformed. In short, there is no better way to learn about what is and is not true for you than to write.

What Do You Have to Do to Write a Book?

Anyone can write a book. The trick is to write a good book. So long as you are honest and true to yourself, you have what it takes to write a good book.

Writing demands that you:

1. Study the craft
2. Give over vast swatches of time and deep emotion to an endeavor with absolutely no guarantee of success
3. Face a blank page or computer screen
4. Face yourself
5. Challenge yourself

Challenges You'll Face along the Way

As a plot consultant, I listen to a lot of fears and flaws that come to the surface of my clients' lives. Because writing is a very personal activity (as well as a very public activity—after all, your intention is to be read by others), a certain intimacy forms between my clients and me during plot consultations. As a result, I've been able to draw lessons about how stories unfold to include the lives of the writers with whom I work.

The following four challenges can stall a writer's enthusiasm to write.

Challenge 1: Procrastination

Not every writer admits to having flaws. Many do. But here's what's really interesting: writers' most prevalent personal flaws operate exactly like the flaws they create in their protagonists.

Writers believe they are not good enough or are too good, not smart enough or too smart, don't produce enough work or produce too much. These uncertainties do more to sabotage you (and your protagonist) from achieving your goals than any outside force ever will.

Writing lifts you and connects you to a higher truth. Temporary feelings of euphoria sweep over you. You are at peace . . . until suddenly, for no apparent reason, you feel lost, abandoned, alone, and stretched beyond your limits. Your goal of writing suddenly seems unattainable.

You become angry, frustrated, disappointed, and ashamed. You have no place to hide, and so, rather than face that blank page and failure, you find other things to do and put off the most important task: your writing.

Challenge 2: Not All Writers Are Created Equal

Writing a story is about creating rich and complex moments, and then stringing those moments together in timely succession. These two tasks call upon the two sides of your brain. When the two sides are balanced and working together, the brain manufactures a realistic, honest story.

Writers in whom the right- and left-brain hemispheres are equal have the natural ability to write a story. Writers with strengths in one hemisphere and weaknesses in the other will excel in some areas of writing a story and falter with other aspects.

THE WRITER'S WAY

This book is not a guide to the brain. This is a book about plotting that also functions as a spiritual or an emotional guide to writing. Writing is emotional. You face obstacles that unleash angst, which leads to procrastination.

My intention in shining a light on how the two hemispheres of the brain affect your writing is to allow you to acknowledge and face the difficulties you encounter, difficulties that are reflections of your strengths and weaknesses. In self-knowledge comes the courage to compensate for your weaknesses and the ability to rely on your strengths.

After all, you, too, are on a heroine's (or hero's) journey. Growth and transformation are available to you as well.

TWO TYPES OF WRITERS

The two sides of the brain process information in different ways, and the two work intimately with each other in just about every action we undertake. The following two types of writers reflect strengths in one of the two complementary cerebral hemispheres.

- Analytical, detail-oriented, bottom-up, left-brained writers think in language more than pictures and begin writing in the turbo thrust of high action and intrigue.
- Intuitive, big-picture, top-down, right-brained writers think in pictures more than language and begin writing by developing characters and moments rich with sensations, thoughts, emotions, and physiological responses.

Broadly speaking, of these two main categories, analytical, detail-oriented (left-brained) writers tend to prefer writing dramatic action. Left-brained writers approach writing in a linear fashion and see the story in its parts. Action-driven writers like structure. Because they like to pre-plot and create an outline before writing, they often refer to themselves as "plotters." They have little trouble expressing themselves in words.

Right-brained writers who fall in the intuitive, big-picture group generally prefer writing about characters and their emotional development. These writers like to use their intuition to work things out on the page, and they abhor pre-plotting and outlining. Character-driven writers often call themselves "pantsers," because of their ability to write by the seats of their pants. They have little trouble expressing feelings. They have the valuable ability to see the story as a whole, even if they have not worked out its details.

When I discovered the two categories of writers, I uncovered a big clue to why some writers—action-driven writers—cling to the plot and structure concepts I offer, whereas others—character-driven writers—display a visceral aversion to plotting.

Balance serves a story well. If you have a firm understanding of what the protagonist wants, you're more likely to have a solid front story. And the front story's dramatic action plot is what makes the reader turn the pages. When characters' goals conflict, they generate excitement on the page.

But an exciting action piece is not enough. Stories also convey a clear idea of how the character embodies human emotional development. A focus on character increases reader identification; your readers connect to your characters on an emotional as well as a rational level.

Challenge 3: Discipline and Structure

Whether you prefer writing action-driven stories or lean toward character-focused tales, you'll find it easiest to maintain discipline in your writing habits if you set goals for yourself.

Left-brained writers usually have little difficulty with the first part of this challenge. Besides creating goals for their characters, they set goals for themselves and devise a schedule to achieve them. At the same time, because they are logical and linear writers, they quickly find confusing the random and chaotic ways a story sometimes presents itself in its generative stage. Left-brained writers often have difficulty in putting pen to paper to get this seemingly random material in front of them.

Once the material is on the page in some form, the action-driven writer walks fully into the power of his or her muse. Left-brain writers have little difficulty in organizing the scenes for greatest impact. At this stage a left-brain writer faces two big hurdles:

1. A lack of knowledge about the craft of bringing a character to life
2. An inner critic who repeatedly censors what they have written

Right-brained writers, on the other hand, pride themselves on being visionaries, capable of carrying in their minds the big pictures of their stories. The force for getting the story down on the page seems to come from outside of them. They have little trouble translating into prose the visions, ideas, dreams, and inspiration that flow into their fertile imaginations. For this reason, right-brained writers often shine during the generative stage.

However, these same big-picture writers struggle when it comes to creating tangible, concrete goals both for their characters and for themselves. When the time comes for right-brained writers to pull together the story for the first rewrite, they quickly bog down. The greatest hurdles at this stage for a right-brained writer to overcome are:

1. To create structure for her story
2. To manage the same inner critic who confronts a left-brained writer

Challenge 4: The Going-Back-to-the-Beginning Syndrome

Many writers, confronted with challenges and uncertainty, refrain from pushing forward. Instead, they go back to the beginning and start over. They justify this by saying, "Well, the story wasn't any good; the characters weren't working; I didn't know where the story was going." Although that may be true to an extent, you need to see it for what it is: an excuse. When the drama and emotion of crafting more and more of the story frightens you, it's tempting to return to the safety of the beginning. Succumb to this challenge and chances are good you will end up in a seemingly never-ending cycle—writing a bit, throwing it out and starting over, writing some more, going back and changing it . . . and so on, forever.

Why Writers Go Back to the Beginning

1. The beginning of the project is introductory. Because it presents the reader with the setting, the characters, the mood, the issues, and all the other important dynamics of the story, it necessarily

skims the surface. Writing and plotting the beginning of a story are like meeting people for the first time. We wonder if the other people like us. We wonder if we like them. We show only so much of ourselves, as we determine how we feel about these other persons. We are in control—and being in control at the beginning sounds far superior to being out of control in the middle and the end, places where you must dig deeply into emotions.

2. In the middle of a story, things get messy as the relationships between the characters develop. Scenes show them as they truly are—warts and all. For writers who like things nice and neat, the middle is an uncomfortable place to linger for very long. It's much nicer to go back to familiar territory.

3. Going back over what you have already written is easier than coming up with something entirely new.

4. The beginning is only a quarter of the page count. The middle of the story makes up half of the entire page count. This requires you to generate twice as many scenes for the middle as for the beginning or for the end. Each scene in the middle shows on a progressively deeper level who the character truly is. That means you have to subject your protagonist to tougher and tougher challenges.

5. The energy throughout the middle is more intense than in the beginning, as the protagonist is more rigorously blocked from reaching her goals.

6. As we'll see later in this book, bad things happen to your characters in the middle. They may be hurt, betrayed, or lost. They may become angry or vindictive. People may walk over them, pounce on them, or do other more gruesome things. If you're in love with your characters, you'll instinctively be reluctant to let any of these things happen to them.

In the middle of the story, masks fall away and the characters reveal themselves, their flaws, fears, judgments, and all. Fights can ensue between characters . . . and between the characters and you. Feelings get hurt. Because few people like confrontations, you back away, afraid of what the characters will reveal, both about themselves and about you. You doubt your ability to manage the dark sides of your characters.

In real life, many of us shy away from disaster and drastic upheaval in order to protect ourselves from deep loss in our own lives. Because of our intimate relationships with the characters we create on the page, we cannot bear to treat them differently. Yet, that is exactly what *must* happen in the story: a crisis. The protagonist's world shatters. Only out of the ashes of the old self can a new self arise—the beginning of the character's ultimate transformation.

In the thick of the middle part of the story, you long for the good old days at the beginning when things were smooth, happy, and superficial. The true nature of the relationships and the characters emerges in the middle. An internal antagonist (the belief that going back and starting again is beneficial) is striving to prevent you from achieving an external goal (finishing your story).

Overcoming Challenge 1: Procrastination

Leave the drama on the page and keep writing. All writers feel uncertain. Turning something as vaporous as inspiration into words that add up to something meaningful is not an easy task. You have every right to doubt your abilities.

When asked about his writing process, Jonathan Evison, author of the *New York Times* bestseller *West of Here,* spoke about a friend of his who took eight years to write one book. Evison, on the other hand, researched and wrote his historical novel in three years and started work on another novel. I appreciate that sometimes stories can take a long time to germinate, but while that is happening, if you are not also writing, you are procrastinating.

If you find yourself plagued with writer's block, chances are you suffer a deeper malady—procrastination. If you find yourself putting off even starting to write, chances are your malady runs deeper still—perfectionism.

Wallow in fear of how a scene will turn out and you will find your-self unable to write. Anxiety over the scene causes you to resist writing the next scene. Anxiety builds to fear and escalates to outright panic. Rather than moving deeper into the story, you stay too long in the safety of an earlier scene. When you do that, your energy fades.

THE WRITER'S WAY

What are you afraid of? That someone will stumble across a rough draft and label you an idiot for the mess? This is not the time to give power to your ego. Writing is a sacred ritual. You act as the messenger for the muse. Let the words flow. Accept imperfection in yourself and you learn to allow for it in others.

Writing a "slop-on-the-page" rough draft is preferable to never writing anything. For a writer to truly call herself a writer, she has to write! She must finish what she starts.

Transform a piece of the invisible world into a visible form. Let it come, one draft at a time.

My advice is, don't worry. You will be given ample time in the process of writing to exercise your craving for perfection—just not yet. The first few drafts set the foundation. The time to fiddle with the details comes later. As soon as the plot and structure work, your focus can turn to making every word, phrase, and metaphor perfect.

Getting Started

I've purposely refrained from giving any advice about where and how to begin your story. If you are one of the lucky ones, perhaps you know the exact right starting place. For the rest of us, faced with the over-whelming task of writing an entire novel, memoir, or screenplay, the most important work at hand is simply to begin. Spending hours of time searching for that elusive perfect starting place is a waste.

Start writing whatever words come to you. Allow for the words to be less than perfect. The real act of writing is not about the rough draft (or at least, mostly not about the rough draft). It's about refining your story through the second and third drafts.

Once you've completed your first draft, however imperfect, you can stand back and, with a new and more realistic perspective, evaluate where and how best to begin the story.

The exercise in the Plot Whisper on the facing page, as well as the one below, is designed to use your strengths to overcome your weaknesses, so both sides of your brain participate together and enhance the writing process.

When you find yourself procrastinating rather than writing, or wondering whether to quit, you have three choices:

1. Keep going and later share your triumph, so others can learn from your mistakes and celebrate your awakening.
2. Turn away from the challenge in front of you and remain unchanged.

PLOT WHISPER

In a journal you designate specifically for the work you will do throughout this book, write a couple of sentences for each of the alternatives listed above and include its consequences.

Make notes about the demands required of you to write a story all the way to the end and how it will feel to complete a story for others to read. Add an example of something you have taken all the way to completion and how it felt to accomplish your goal.

Beneath that, jot down what you say to yourself and others about giving up your writing and how you will feel without having writing in your life. Describe an endeavor you quit and how you feel now about having done that.

Next, write a scenario about starting a story and not finishing, but also not giving up. What will that feel like? What activity in your life is playing out like that now?

3. Linger for months, years, or even a lifetime in limbo, neither going forward nor ever being able to fully go back.

A deep yearning and determination will serve you better than either skill or knowledge and give you the strength to choose the first alternative.

Overcoming Challenge 2: Not All Writers Are Created Equal

Identify your strengths and weaknesses. Do you:

- Crave action? (a left-brained writer preference)
- Spew out dialogue at will? (a left-brained writer preference)
- Fall in love with your characters? (a right-brained writer preference)
- Ponder themes and meaning? (a right-brained writer preference)
- All of the above? (a writer with a balanced brain)

To follow are descriptions of plot consultations with two vastly different writers. One writer typifies classic behaviors for left-brain dominance and the other writer for right-brain dominance. As you read, identify which abilities you possess. Note whether your answers indicate a preference for one side of your brain over the other.

Writer Number One is a man who's constructed a logical, well-thought-out, and detailed dramatic action plot. He's arranged the different parts of his story—scenes and chapters—in a clear sequence. Based on his writing preferences, it's clear he draws heavily from the left half of his brain.

The plot consultation with Writer Number One progresses clearly and quickly as he recounts logically constructed details and the parts of an action-driven story he imagines. Throughout the two hours of our session, I gently probe for the meaning of the story. Not until close to the end of the consultation do I fully grasp the theme of his overall story. Only at this point does he realize what he's been trying to say through his plot. Though he's examined many of the big action chunks, the coherence and meaning are muddled, and his characters are undeveloped.

In the end, thanks to the plot planner visual aid (see Introduction), we unravel the plot and see it as a whole. It's clear that for him, characterization and emotion are weaknesses that he'll have to overcome.

Writer Number Two is a woman with a wildly creative premise and lots of random ideas for an overall story. Based on our conversation, I determine she draws from the right side of her brain.

She has no trouble describing the big picture of her story. She knows all about her themes and the emotions she wants to evoke in the reader. But as the consultation progresses and I ask her about the details—what to put where—she has difficulty explaining her intentions. Her story has a sensational twist, but she cannot see a logical way to get there. This is not the first time she has come to me for help in outlining her story. Even after two successfully published novels, she needs help in creating a linear structure for her work.

In talking about her story, she flits from one scene idea to another, in no clear sequence. Then she moves out of the scenes to speak broadly about the overall plot. I continually bring her back to the details.

These two examples—and there are hundreds more I could mention—should give you an idea of the challenges you will face. It's important from the beginning to identify your strengths and weaknesses. It helps to know if you're good at plotting but weak at conveying character emotion. Perhaps your strength is in creating quirky and likeable characters, but you have trouble giving a sense of coherence to your story. Knowing these things prepares you to better meet the challenges ahead with a spirit of discovery.

Overcoming Challenge 3: Discipline and Structure

Compensate for your weaknesses/embrace your strengths. Writing forces you to come face-to-face with your weaknesses. Rather than allowing your weaknesses to slowly erode your passion for your story as challenges reveal themselves, face them head-on.

The rhythm of storytelling is in everyone, especially for those who were read to as youngsters and who continue to read fiction today. Natural-born storytellers tap into this rhythm unconsciously and are able to interweave dramatic action with character development to create a thematically significant story. Often such writers do this without much conscious thought about structure and development.

PLOT WHISPER

Here are some tips to help action-driven writers strengthen reader identification with your characters:

To make your protagonist more human, give her a flaw of your own, a fear, and/or a secret. We all have them, which explains why a flawed character is more appealing to readers and moviegoers than is a character who is perfect.

Next to your computer, tack up a list of flaws shared by you and your protagonist. Change or add to the traits as you write and come to know your characters (and yourself) better. The longer you work, the deeper you will dig and the more significant your story becomes.

Look for opportunities to incorporate thematic patterning, metaphors, and analogies into your writing (I'll give you some more exercises in Chapters Four and Eleven).

Look for opportunities to role-play. Pretend to be your protagonist confronting challenging situations. Use those experiences to write action scenes that include true character behavior and emotion.

Periodically, stop writing, get up from your computer, and move your body. The more in touch you are with your body, the better able you are to write about physical reactions as well as sensation and emotions.

For the rest of us it's not so easy. Often our stories turn out lopsided. We concentrate solely on our strengths, whether that's strong linear development or theme and character. The result is a story that feels unbalanced.

For example, left-brained writers too often concentrate only on action scenes. But no matter how exciting the action, these scenes usually neglect the human element. Such an omission increases your chances of losing your audience's interest.

By contrast, right-brained writers tilt toward the inner workings of their characters and away from the external conflict and tension that are needed to build suspense. They neglect dramatic action, which makes up the front story and gets the reader turning the pages.

A writer tends to process and use information from her dominant side. A firm commitment to face your weaknesses is not enough. You, also, must learn to compensate for them.

PLOT WHISPER

Here are some tips for character-driven writers:

Use goals of your own and insert them into the context of the story.

Writers who focus on their characters' emotions tend to embrace a more random writing style and rebel against structured plot planners. You benefit from seeing, feeling, and touching real objects. Instead of using words to identify the scenes on a plot planner, tape up pictures clipped from magazines (or draw images yourself) to represent the character(s) and the action in each scene.

The right side of the brain is color sensitive. Shape- and color-coded sticky notes on your plot planner help. Assign each character a different color. Pick a shape to represent the dramatic action and another shape to point out thematic elements.

You may already have a vision of how the protagonist is transformed at the end. Start at the climax of your story and work backward. Using your intuition, pay attention to coherence and meaning as you generate action scene ideas. Link dramatic action to the changes in your characters' emotional development.

Schedule a walk during your writing time. As you walk, imagine yourself plotting out your next five scenes in sequence according to the action they embody. The act of seeing yourself plotting will help you actually do it when you return to your writing.

You like to back up everything visually, so hang your plot planner on a wall near your computer. This will help you remember the sequence of your story as you write and rewrite.

Writers who are weak at developing complex characters are often good list makers, skilled at thinking in sequence. If you're one of these people, you may benefit from showing your character's emotional growth in linear form on a plot planner that is separate from the dramatic action plot planner (Chapter Three shows you how to do this).

Compare the dramatic action plot planner to the character emotional development plot planner. Look for clues to how the dramatic action causes changes in the character's emotional development and how the character's choices change the dramatic action.

Overcoming Challenge 4: The Going-Back-to-the-Beginning Syndrome

Push forward. The further you put yourself out there with your writing the more vulnerable you feel. It is risky to follow the energy of your story out of your comfort zone. Always, the choice to delve deeper into the Universal Story represents a leap of faith and a belief in the journey's potential for growth.

Write the book all the way to the end first. Then go back and see what you have.

Five Reasons to Push Through the Middle of the Story

1. Until you write the entire story, you do not know the end. And until you write the end—the climax—you do not know what belongs in the beginning.
2. You accomplish what you set out to do.
3. With a skeleton in place, you are able to stand back and see the story in an entirely new light.
4. The less time you devote to making every word perfect in the first couple of drafts the less painful future cuts and revisions will be. Because you haven't invested hundreds of hours going back to the beginning, you'll be less reluctant to cut the customary thirty-five to 100 pages that almost always get chopped from the beginning of the manuscript. The more of yourself you give to making every word perfect before moving to the next scene, the more emotionally attached you become to the words. Cutting your work is never easy, but the more you can endure the chaos of ugly prose, gaps, and missteps in the early drafts, the better.
5. One of the greatest benefits of writing a truly awful, lousy, no good first draft is that it can only get better from there.

The Emotional Rewards of Writing

I believe that writing is not a gift but a skill—a skill based on self-esteem. To become a good writer involves creating a healthy sense of self, which becomes simpler when you are fully aware of both your strengths and your weaknesses as a writer.

While writing you are not always in the flow of your strength. The real magic lies waiting in that which you resist (fear) the most. If you hate (fear) showing character emotion, your story improves the instant you focus your full attention on the task and make the attempt. If you despise (fear) the idea of imposing structure on your story, your writing life shifts when you take steps toward that end.

The better you know yourself and the broader your understanding of the universality of the story of your life, the less resistance and pain you experience when crafting a story. Understanding the universality and interconnectedness of everyone's stories allows you to appreciate the forces that both support and interfere with your success.

The deeper you delve into this book, the more you will recognize the universal components in your work—your protagonist's emotions in a scene, your reaction to situations, and the significance of friends and foes in your story and in your life.

The more conscious you are of the meaning of your writing and your story, the closer attention you pay to the words you write, the schedules you create, and the language you speak.

When you move from talking about writing a book, a screenplay, or your memoir to actually doing it, you join your destiny. Once you begin, there is no turning back. The act of writing changes you. The transformation has already begun.

PART ONE

THE OUTLINE OF THE PLOT: STARTING IS HALF THE BATTLE

CHAPTER TWO
THE UNIVERSAL STORY

Language is the most imperfect and expensive means yet discovered for communicating thought.

—William James

Writers write for as many reasons as there are stories and writers. The stories we tell originate from outside ourselves. It is as if the muse, in search of a conduit, plugs into our imaginations. Most people who analyze writing would argue that the impulse to write comes from within, and that writers write what they know, what's part of their own experience, which they externalize and transform in the process of externalizing it. I believe that the fragment of a dream or wisp of inspiration that urges you to sit down and write offers you the exact right story needed to activate not only your own personal transformation but the reader's as well.

A belief in the partnership between the writer and the Universal Story makes you less inclined to give full ownership of the story to your ego. This partnership helps you do what needs to be done for the good of the story and readies you to work in concert within yourself and outside yourself.

You listen to a stirring deep inside you. You imagine yourself as a successful writer. You see yourself winning prizes, making lots of

21

money, and speaking on talk shows. You earn enough in royalties to quit your day job.

Let me stop you there.

First, you have to write the book.

The Kinds of Stories We Tell

Whatever their form, all stories at their core follow the same basic pattern as does nature. Life is born, expands, and then contracts and closes, only to begin again. In the same way, the energy of all stories ebbs and flows along the way.

THE WRITER'S WAY

Writers often ask how long it takes to write a book. The time is mostly determined by the writer's degree of resistance. To succeed, you have to tolerate failure. Risks are involved and sacrifices required. What you must determine is: How much do you want it? This is true of science-fiction stories, comedies, epics, action-adventure, horror and thrillers, crime stories, westerns, fantasies, children's books, young adult, picture books, romance, erotic, sports stories, historical novels, and memoirs. What varies is the rhythm of these ebbs and flows.

STYLES OF STORYTELLING

Some stories move quickly with page-turning action and suspense, such as the Academy Award–winning screenplay and story *The Fighter* by Scott Silver, Paul Tamasy, Eric Johnson, and Keith Dorrington. Other stories, such as Anne Tyler's Pulitzer Prize–winning novel *Breathing Lessons*, meander around the study of a character's emotional development. Some novels ponder profound ideas, as does *The Elegance of the Hedgehog* by Muriel Barbery with its philosophical passages and ruminations. Other stories showcase the cadence of the author's writing and the beauty of her language, for example, the National Book Award-winning memoir *Just Kids* by Patti Smith.

THE UNIVERSAL STORY AND ITS IMPORTANCE

In all these cases, there is a common structure beneath the stories. Writers benefit from studying this structure, also known as the Universal Story.

The Universal Story is the story of life. Since before time was recorded, it has been transforming simple words into masterpieces. From humankind's earliest days, those who told stories were invited to sit close to the fire and were offered the largest portions of food. Their stories, passed on and remembered, struck a primordial chord. That early form of the Universal Story remains consistent today and replicates the four-click rhythm of a mother's heartbeat that newborns yearn for. It's found in the regular and predictable pattern of the song sung by the humpback whale. Tap into the Universal Story and better direct the flow of your story to connect with your readers on a deep and profound level.

The Structure of the Universal Story

The energy of the Universal Story flows through three phases:

- Comfort and Separation
- Resistance and Struggle
- Transformation and Return

The Beginning—Comfort and Separation

Whether it's in a novel or in a life, beginnings form the foundation upon which everything else rests. Beginnings, though fragile, embody great heart and hope. The beginnings of stories follow clearly definable elements of introduction and grounding.

INTRODUCTION

In the first quarter of a story, the three major plots of the story are introduced. These three are dramatic action, character emotional development, and thematic significance: the who, the what, and the why.

In the beginning of *Lord of the Flies*, author William Golding introduces a character emotional development plot. The protagonist, we learn, is Ralph, a lighthearted, curious, and kind boy. Golding gives us a glimpse of the other British schoolboys stranded with Ralph on the island, showing a bit of the major characters' emotional and psychological makeup. The dramatic action plot is launched with the central dilemma: a group of young boys have been marooned on a tropical island bereft of adult supervision and are waiting to be rescued. Along with the dramatic development of the story, Golding presents the reader with a thematic plot that discusses how a defective society can be traced back to defects in human nature. He sounds this theme with the comment, " . . . people are never quite what you thought they were."

GROUNDING

In the first quarter of a story, the writer also introduces the when and the where. A firm sense of the story's time frame and setting grounds the reader. Details about the period and place send the reader even deeper.

National Book Award–winning author Tim O'Brien begins *July, July,* "The reunion dance had started only an hour ago." He follows with a glimpse into the gossip and confessions under way at Minnesota's Darton Hall College as two of the major characters reveal their emotional development by what they say about the murder of a classmate.

They fell quiet then, sipping vodka, watching the class of '69 rediscover itself on a polished gymnasium dance floor. Unofficially, this
was a thirtieth reunion—one year tardy due to someone's over-
sight . . .

The beginning quarter of *July, July* shows ten old friends reassem-
bled three decades after their graduation and hints at the conflicts of
the generation launched into adulthood at the moment when their
country, too, lost its innocence.

This is where we stand at the beginning of the story. The characters
have been assembled, their goals have been defined, and the theme of
the story has been anticipated. The location of the story has been established as well as the time frame, both immediate—night or day—and
broad—the season, year, or era.

Beginnings are times of grandiose dreams of escape, success, change,
and possibilities. This is true not only for the protagonist of your story,
but also for you.

PARAMETERS OF THE BEGINNING

Writers often stay too long in the introductory phase of the beginning. This is understandable. You warm up at the beginning. You get
to know your characters. You find yourself telling all sorts of important
backstory details about the characters and the story. At least, you think
they're important.

There is nothing wrong with this in the first draft. In subsequent
drafts, you'll need to cut this introduction to a reasonable length and
prune those details down to the essentials of what the reader *needs to
know* in order to get on with the story. If, in the second, third, or fourth
draft you find yourself still rambling on about details, you have a significant problem.

By going on too long in the beginning, you risk alienating your
reader. Your audience grows tired of the introductions and wants something big to happen. They're impatient to get to the "good part," the

heart of the story itself. Bluntly, no one is interested in your characters until they do something interesting.

At the same time, beginnings that are less than one-quarter of the entire scene count give the reader too little information, leaving him or her inadequately prepared to proceed confidently into the rest of the story.

Introduce one character at a time, beginning with the protagonist. Give the reader a chance to become grounded in the style of the story, to become familiar with the setting, and to focus on the main character. Readers can easily become overwhelmed when you introduce too many characters at once, forcing them to retain lots of specific information up front.

The beginning of your story should accomplish the following goals:

- Establish the story's time and place.
- Set up the dramatic action and the underlying conflict that will run throughout the story.
- Introduce the major characters, giving the reader an idea of who they are, their emotional makeup, and the weight they carry in the story.
- Allude to the theme.
- Introduce the protagonist's short-term goal and give a hint, at least, of her long-term goal.

Each of these elements, which you present in the first quarter of the story, establishes a contract between you and your readers. It tells them what you promise your story is about and alerts them to the limitations of your story—it's *about* some things and *not about* others.

How to Deal with the Backstory at the Beginning

Here's a basic rule from the Plot Whisperer: Don't tell a character's backstory until the readers have had a chance to know him. All the pain and suffering, unfair treatment, family drama, and the other horrible things that happened to the protagonist in the past—if you tell that in the first quarter of a story before readers have a chance to care about the character, you'll put them off. Your reader may feel empathy for your protagonist's past. More likely she's looking for excuses to stop reading and put the book away.

In the first quarter of the story, you are inviting the reader to develop a relationship with your protagonist. Just as when you meet someone for the first time, begin by showing the character on her best behavior. Show off her strengths. Hint at her weaknesses and flaws, but keep them in the background. This gives the reader time to get to know and like the protagonist. As the reader becomes comfortable with the character, she is more apt to endure the protagonist's flaws, fears, and prejudices, and to forgive her when she reveals the darker side of herself.

If you don't keep the backstory vague in the beginning, it makes your decision about where to begin your story more difficult. I've heard writers offer excuses such as:

- "I know all their history, so why would I want to withhold it from the reader?"
- "I wrote it that way."
- "It's the good part."

Writers spend lots of time imagining and writing every detail of a character's past, from childhood to maturity. Rather than share everything right away and demonstrate how clever you are, consider instead how curiosity works.

THE POWER OF CURIOSITY

Curiosity draws the reader deeper into the story world. Give away everything up front and you lose that.

Let's consider the Pulitzer Prize–winning novel *Beloved* by Toni Morrison. In the first chapter the reader learns that the house in which the protagonist, Sethe, lives with her daughter, Denver, is haunted. The reader also learns about the catastrophic events years earlier that caused

Sethe, a slave, to run away from a farm in Kentucky. However, the only other information Morrison gives the reader is that Sethe's oldest daughter is the ghost haunting the house and that she died after having her throat slit. In order to learn why and who did the despicable act, the reader is drawn further and further into the story. By the time the facts behind the awful murder are revealed, more than halfway through the novel, the reader has grown to care so intensely for Sethe that he viscerally feels the horror of what happened.

The longer you wait to deliver the full backstory, the explanation of what in the past made the character who she or he is today, the greater the impact of the revelation. The moment when the protagonist lost her balance often occurs years before the story begins. But there's no reason to always start from that point.

Writers try all sorts of devices to highlight that moment. Flashback is among the most common, along with summary (which can get very clumsy very fast) and dumping details of the character's past into dialogue. Resist the urge to cram everything about your characters into the beginning. What you leave out is as important as what stays in.

When a character appears in a scene at the beginning of the story, give the reader only enough about the character to inform that particular scene. Hold back any information that is not essential. Do not tease your readers, but don't overload them with information either. Instead, invite them to read on, to find out what happens next. As they proceed, they'll come to understand the characters and why they act as they do. But don't race to get to that point.

My recommendation regarding flashbacks is, wait until the middle. Flashbacks, especially early in a story, create time disorientation. They're a useful technique if done well (*Lost Horizon* by James Hilton is one long flashback with two short bookends at the beginning and end of the novel), but they're better placed in the middle of the story.

HOW TO INCORPORATE THE BACKSTORY INTO THE BEGINNING

Sometimes, despite what I've just said, your plot demands that you incorporate a certain amount of backstory in the beginning of the book. If that's the case—and you should only do it after looking long and hard at whether it's really necessary—here are some tips on how to do it effectively.

The best way to approach this problem is through the nuances of setting, time frame, physical details, and dialogue. You can inject back-story information through word choices, mood, tone, actions, and reactions. The worst way is through a kind of generalized information dump, which is simultaneously boring and overwhelming. (Though not always. The opening chapters of *The Girl With the Dragon Tattoo*, which I'll discuss later in a different context, are one giant information dump. In that case, against all expectations, it works.)

Toni Morrison handles backstory brilliantly in the multitude of ways she informs her readers in the early sections of her novel *Beloved*. For example, in the first chapter Sethe offers Paul D., a slave from the Kentucky farm she has not seen in years, a chance to stay the night.

"You don't sound too steady in the offer."

Sethe glanced beyond his shoulder toward the closed door. "Oh it's truly meant . . ."

Paul D. starts to follow Sethe through the door and steps "straight into a pool of red and undulating light that locked him where he stood."

"You got company?" he whispered, frowning.

"Off and on," said Sethe.

"Good God." He backed out the door onto the porch. "What kind of evil you got in here?"

"It's not evil, just sad. Come on. Just step through."

Sethe's glance beyond Paul D.'s shoulder, her vague answer to his query about having company, and her explanation that what Paul D. senses is not evil but sadness, shows her uncertainty about whether Paul

D. by entering the house will reignite the dormant ghost (who represents Sethe's true backstory). It also suggests the tenor of the scene—not terror but sorrow.

Stages of Separation

In the beginning quarter of the story, get the front story going first by hooking readers and audiences with present moment-to-moment conflict. The protagonist faces an immediate dilemma, experiences a loss, feels fear, and is compelled to take action.

For instance, let's consider John Steinbeck's Pulitzer Prize–winning novel, *The Grapes of Wrath*. Tom Joad is introduced merely as a hitchhiker intent on getting a ride. That immediate goal is answered when he convinces a truck driver to give him a ride despite the driver's "No Riders" sticker on the windshield. The reader is curious why the hitchhiker wears all new clothes, though the coat is too big and the trousers are too short, and especially when the driver who picks him up tells the hitchhiker, "You oughtn' to take no walk in new shoes—hot weather." The hiker replies defensively, "Guy got to wear 'em if he got no others." That exchange alone tells us something about Joad's poverty as well as his practicality.

The protagonist embarks on a transformational journey, not to gain something new but to regain what was lost as represented in the backstory. Rather than show the backstory in a scene in the beginning, show what the character is unable to do now due to flawed beliefs. The middle of the story then becomes a journey to relearn or reattain a skill or knowledge lost, forgotten, or stolen that is necessary for the character to conquer her greatest challenge at the climax. This reconnection to what was lost in the character's backstory always plays out in the Universal Story.

You may have written pages and pages about your protagonist's backstory and are impatient to share the details with the reader. You force yourself to write the dramatic action scenes the protagonist takes in the beginning of the story. When you find yourself, after every scene, wishing to share the past information about the character, remember that some of the most lasting stories treat the protagonist's backstory in the beginning in less than a paragraph, sometimes merely a sentence— including *The Grapes of Wrath*, *To Kill a Mockingbird*, *A Lesson Before Dying*, and *The Great Gatsby*.

Ask yourself if the backstory *is* the story. If so, write that story. If not, write the front story first. Then decide where and how to present the background information about the characters.

Remember that keeping the backstory vague allows the reader to actively participate in the story by filling in the missing blanks. Hold back the character's backstory, at least until you write the entire first draft and are able to assess the story you are telling.

The End of the Beginning

In 1942, at a turning point in World War II, Prime Minister Winston Churchill, in a speech to Parliament, said, "Now, this is not the end. It is not even the beginning of the end. But it is, perhaps, the end of the beginning."

You choose to devote yourself to your writer's journey more deeply when you actually begin writing. This forward movement signifies that the beginning phase is finished. You have crossed over into the world of the story itself and entered the exotic new stage of fully becoming a writer.

In the same way in fiction, something happens to make the protagonist's old world contract and no longer fit. The end of the beginning represents a break from the old world order as the character embarks on a journey into an exotic new world.

To return to our earlier example, the end of the beginning of *Lord of the Flies* occurs when the protagonist, Ralph, is unable to convince the antagonist, Jack, to give up his goal of killing a pig and commit to a goal of building a shelter and feeding the fire for rescue.

A fracture between the two of them is wide enough that when they leave the old world, "all the warm salt water of the bathing pool and the shouting and splashing and laughing were only just sufficient to bring them together again."

The Middle—Resistance and Struggle

When the character enters the middle of the story, she is confronted with a new and strange world that is fertile ground for expansion.

The more unusual the new world, surroundings, mind-set, and demands of the middle, the more exotic are the experiences, explorations, endurance, and quest for survival. In the exotic new world, the old rules and beliefs no longer apply.

On page one of *Lord of the Flies*, Ralph is thrust into the world of a deserted island with no adult supervision. Still, throughout the beginning quarter of the story, he is the same boy he always was—laughing, turning somersaults, instilling trust among the other boys, and jerking up "his stockings with an automatic gesture that made the jungle seem for a moment like the Home Countries." In the beginning, Ralph, as always, is liked and respected.

When the story crosses from the beginning quarter into the middle, the already alien world turns dark and threatening. Ralph quickly finds "once more that evening [he] had to adjust his values."

The new world deals in opposites—rapture and anguish, light and shadow, ego and unity, good and evil. Antagonists, both external and internal, emerge from every angle in the middle of the story. These obstacles can be human or non-human. Other challenges originate in the character herself, in other people's fears and judgments, and in the rules of society.

Halfway Point

The halfway point in the Universal Story represents the next major turning point.

In the middle of *Lord of the Flies*, Ralph loses hope. He thinks, "I ought to give up being chief . . ." Instead, he forces the boys on the island to recommit to his plan of keeping the fire lighted as a rescue beacon.

The boys come to believe that the island is inhabited by a beast. Ralph insists they search the only place the phantom beast could be hiding. "If the beast isn't there we'll go up the mountain and look; and light the fire."

The Crisis

Often, before the true road appears, failure, brokenness, fear, emptiness, and alienation cause suffering and loss. The only way to re-creation lies through death. First, the old must be destroyed.

THE WRITER'S WAY

After the crisis, the protagonist picks herself up and moves steadily toward the climax. The writer, however, has free will. Staggering from metaphorical pain and death, you enter a threshold. Your decision about which way to go next narrows down to two choices:

1. Resist what is and become a victim.
2. Yield to what is and become a victor.

Stripped of everything at the crisis, you clearly see your protagonist's story mirrors your own.

Tension and conflict steadily rise to the breaking point. In *Lord of the Flies* the "bigun" boys and the "littluns" turn into a mob. The dramatic action plot presents the crisis as a ritual frenzy in which the boys stab Simon to death and stone Piggy.

The End—Transformation and Return

After the crisis, the energy of the story turns down briefly, and then expands. The pieces of the story begin to form a bigger picture.

Ralph, in *Lord of the Flies*, clearly sees that what the boys have done—stabbing Simon—is murder. "I'm frightened," he cries. "Of us. I want to go home. Oh God, I want to go home."

The end begins when the protagonist takes the final steps necessary for the completion of his long-term goal. Stories and lives demand action. Every movement forward signifies that transformation has begun. In both death and rebirth, the pattern repeats itself. Every moment is connected to every other moment.

Ralph, knowing the boys' hope of rescue depends on keeping the signal fire on the island lit continuously, decides he must set out for Jack's camp "to see about the fire" "and about Piggy's specs," which the other group under Jack's leadership has stolen. The crisis, the murder of Simon, impels him to action, his only way forward in the situation.

Climax

Every story rises to a climax. You and your character reconnect with your ultimate destinies. The promise of transformation is realized and released. Well aware of his own inherent savagery, Ralph faces his enemy, Jack, and confronts head-on the beastliness in all of us.

Unable to remind the others of the values of rules, and unwilling to give up the goodness of laws and rescue, Ralph separates from the other boys, now turned fully savage, and runs.

Resolution

The resolution of a story is the sum of the character's actions. It gives the reader a sense of what the story world looks like now that the protagonist has been transformed.

What You Can Learn from the Universal Story

My understanding of the Universal Story and its importance emerged from twenty years of research into the anatomy of stories, consulting with writers, and energy work. By gaining a fluent knowledge of the Universal Story, you gain at least two strengths:

1. The more skilled you are at presenting your words according to the time-honored techniques, the more compelling your story and the stronger its connection will be with readers and audiences.
2. By creating a transformative plot for your story, you improve your productivity as a writer, which in turn transforms the quality of both your writing life and your personal life.

Stand back from the drama of your own life and gain a deeper understanding of the bigger picture by assessing where you currently are in the Universal Story. Determine how your own individual story is related to and is integrated within the whole of your life. Learn about the strength and purpose of your own personal power and what weakens you as a writer and a person. Seize the capacity to create vital stories and live a meaningful life.

The Universal Story is in the undercurrent of every breath you take, every story you tell yourself, and all the stories you write. Learn to refer to it when you arrange a story or when, having written, you find yourself mired and lost or simply curious about where you are and where you are headed or, at least, the general direction in which you are moving.

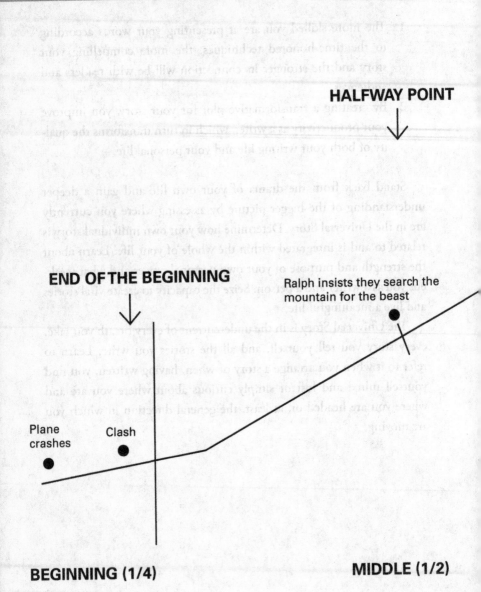

Figure 3. Plot Planner for *Lord of the Flies* by William Golding

HALFWAY POINT

END OF THE BEGINNING

Ralph insists they search the
mountain for the beast

Plane
crashes   Clash

BEGINNING (1/4)   MIDDLE (1/2)

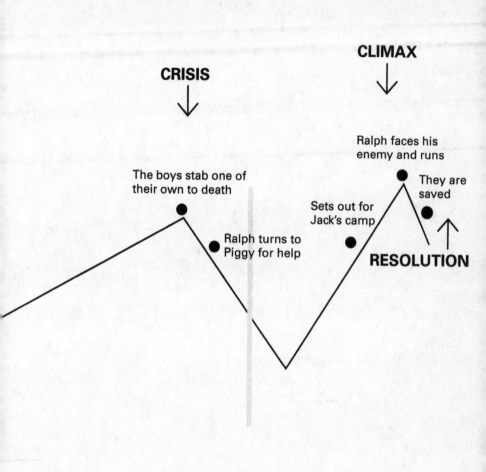

CRISIS

CLIMAX

Ralph faces his
enemy and runs

The boys stab one of
their own to death

They are
saved

Ralph turns to
Piggy for help

Sets out for
Jack's camp

RESOLUTION

END (1/4)

CHAPTER THREE

THE BASICS OF PLOTTING

A story to me means a plot where there is some surprise. Because that's how life is—full of surprises.
—Isaac Bashevis Singer

Early in my career, I sat down at the kitchen table and plotted out classics including *The Grapes of Wrath* and *The Great Gatsby* and *Lord of the Flies* on ten-, twelve-, and twenty-foot strips of butcher paper. It was an enormously useful exercise (one I'd recommend that you try with some of your favorite books). It quickly became apparent to me that plot embodies quite a bit more than the sum of the events in a story. This was the customary definition of plot when I started writing back in the late eighties and early nineties. But I realized that it was wrong.

Plot is how the events in a story directly impact the main charac-ter. Always, in the best-written stories, characters are emotionally affected by the events of the story. In great stories, the dramatic action transforms characters. This transformation makes a story meaningful.

For instance, every event in *To Kill a Mockingbird,* Harper Lee's fifty-year-old classic about the American South, affects Scout's growth and development as she learns to walk in someone else's shoes.

What's a Plot Planner and How Can I Use It?

A plot planner is a visual line that represents the invisible energy of the Universal Story. It enables you to assess the significance of your characters and the dramatic action of your story by seeing how all the scenes work together against the backdrop of the entire piece. Such a multilayered attentiveness to your story allows for a unique perspective into the deeper meaning of your story.

A plot planner gives a visual accounting of all the scenes in a story. It helps you compare scenes that heighten conflict and suspense to those quieter scenes that show the character in control. Each scene delivers more tension and conflict than the preceding scene and builds with intensity to the story's climax. Standing back from all the words and viewing the story as a whole allows you to better determine the causality between scenes and the overall coherence of the story. With such an insight, you are able to turn scenes with emotionally rich characters who are experiencing conflict into the driving force behind an exceptional story.

The plot planner is a visual aid to help you write and finish your project in a way that pleases you and ultimately satisfies your readers, too.

I've heard from many writers that when they hit a rough patch and lose energy for their stories, merely a switch from writing to filling in a template stimulates their creative juices. Before writers know it, they are back to writing.

FUNDAMENTALS OF THE PLOT PLANNER

The number one rule for distilling an abstract concept like plot into a concrete picture is to keep the template simple.

The first time you see a plot planner you may find yourself leaning forward and gazing at the template as if you were looking into the eyes of a long-lost beloved. If this reaction fits you, chances are good you are a linear, left-brained writer and you find the plot planner is a lifesaver. However, if you scowl and fold your arms across your chest, sense yourself turning pale, or feel as if your eyes are popping out of your head, you are probably a right-brained, character-driven writer. If so, no matter how threatening that simple plot planner line feels to you, do not despair. You, too, will come to rely on the plot planner as much as the linear, left-brained, action-driven writers.

PLOT WHISPER

To create a plot planner, draw a line on a six-foot strip of paper. Start near the bottom left corner and draw a solid black line that travels steadily upward to a peak about three-quarters of the way across the paper, then drops down into a valley, quickly ascends to an even higher peak, and ends near the right top edge of the paper in a short, falling line. The line on the paper represents the energetic flow of the Universal Story and is a perfect place to plan a plot.

Later you will arrange the scenes from your story on this plot planner. Above the line, you'll place the scenes with external dramatic action. Below the line will go the scenes that are passive, filled with summary and backstory, or heavy with information.

For now, simply draw the line and look for a place to hang your plot planner so that you pass by it several times a day.

Whichever way you feel about the plot planner, for now, step away from the words of your stories. If you think that's odd advice, it probably is. After all, writers write words. Even so, too many writers hide behind beautiful words and clever turns of phrases and balk at applying structure and plot to their stories.

Eventually, I'll ask you to plot your story on a plot planner so you can see it in its entirety: how the dramatic action scenes flow into a whole, how one scene affects the overall story, and what all the action scenes add up to. For now, concentrate on the visual tool itself. Imagine a plot planner helping you develop and deepen your own individual story.

The plot planner is a place to organize your ideas, your goals, and even your life path. The plot planner also is primarily where you plot out the scenes of your story.

BENEFITS OF WRITING IN SCENES

Before you can create a visual map for analyzing critical story information, presentation flow, and the overall story sequence, you have to have scenes. Likely, you have heard the writer's mantra: "Show, don't tell." Summary tells. Scenes show.

Let's look at a partial scene from the middle-grade Newbery Medal-winning novel *Holes* by Louis Sachar. Stanley Yelnats has been unjustly sent to a boys' detention center where the boys build character by spending all day, every day, digging holes exactly five feet wide and five feet deep.

> [Stanley] glanced helplessly at his shovel. It wasn't defective. He was defective.
>
> He noticed a thin crack in the ground. He placed the point of his shovel on top of it, then jumped on the back of the blade with both feet.
>
> The shovel sank a few inches into the packed earth.
>
> He smiled. For once in his life it paid to be overweight.
>
> He leaned on the shaft and pried up his first shovelful of dirt, then dumped it off to the side.
>
> Only ten million more to go, he thought, then placed the shovel back in the crack and jumped on it again.
>
> He unearthed several shovelfuls of dirt in this manner, before it occurred to him that he was dumping his dirt within the perimeter

of his hole. He laid his shovel flat on the ground and marked where the edges of his hole would be. Five feet was awfully wide.

He moved the dirt he'd already dug up out past his mark. He took a drink from his canteen. Five feet would be awfully deep, too.

This scene, as do all good scenes, shows moment-to-moment action in real story time. The reader experiences the work as Stanley does it and learns about the protagonist, not because the author tells us but because he *shows* us through Stanley's actions. We learn the protagonist is overweight and can laugh at himself. We learn he has staying power because rather than give up and suffer the consequences he finds a way to break the earth open. We learn he is bright in that he quickly realizes his mistake in dumping the dirt within the perimeter of his hole and immediately rectifies the situation.

The details of Stanley jumping on the back of the shovel blade with both feet, leaning on the shaft, measuring the hole, and taking a drink from his canteen draw the reader into the moment of the scene. The reader attaches viscerally to the fleeting happiness Stanley feels at being heavy enough to sink the shovel a few inches into the packed earth, his despondency when he understands how wide five feet actually is, his momentary success in prying up his first shovelful, and his disappointment in counting "only ten million more to go"—not to mention his despair when he acknowledges the full magnitude of the task in front of him.

Living in the present moment can be difficult for most people. Usually our minds dart into the future—whether ten minutes or ten years from now—or back into the past.

Stories are structured as a series of real-time scenes. Watching a scene unfold on the page, we connect to the Universal Story. We walk in the shoes of a character and feel what she feels. Scenes in a story or novel create their own time and the emotional sensation that the present moment is all that exists. Instead of merely reading the words, we sink into the story world and surrender even our emotions to the illusion of the scene. Readers experience this time as the characters in the scene experience it.

This strengthens as we come to know the characters and care for them, even worry about them. Our bodies respond on a visceral level; our hearts beat faster. We laugh and weep because we're involved in the story world itself.

Scenes play out in the *now*. Evoke a true and authentically emotional moment and you have yourself a scene. The practice of writing in scenes becomes a spiritual rite. In the moments you write in scenes, you live in the power of now.

Here are some scene elements that can entice your readers to sink deeper into the story:

- Characters with whom the reader identifies
- Conflict, tension, and suspense that sustain excitement
- Only enough backstory to inform that particular scene
- Clarity about whom and what to cheer and mourn in the story
- Consistency in story pacing
- Strong sensory details
- Enticing foreshadowing
- No author intrusion
- Turning points in the dramatic action and the characters' emotional development

The best stories are those in which we are so involved with the characters and caught up in the moment that we find another five minutes to keep reading. Lured deeper and deeper into the dream, we are unable to wrench ourselves away.

After we close the book, we take a moment or two to remember that the people in the story are an illusion. Often, we must shake ourselves and consciously detach from the pages before we can return to real life.

Each scene has a plot structure of its own. The scene shows the character take a step toward a goal or desire. The scene's moment-by-moment action creates conflict and tension as shown through dialogue, facial expressions, gestures, and every detail of the character's response. The scene ends with failure, an unanswered question, a cliffhanger, a mishap that entices the audience deeper into the story. On the other hand, a scene that shows the character achieving a short-term goal but that fails to transition effectively to the next scene dissipates the story's energy. It's like stepping on a stair that's missing. The reader knows instinctively that something's wrong, sighs, and puts down the book.

Between the Scenes

As important as scenes are, summary has its place in stories, too. In stories that take place over a long time or geographic span, one scene cannot always smoothly move into the next. To avoid the story becoming episodic, you must make creative use of summary. (Also, a story made up only of scenes can inject too much conflict and become exhausting for the reader.) Summary is a place to make transitions. Instead of every single moment played out in scene, a summary compresses time and space.

Summary narrates quickly those events that are not important enough to the overall story line to show in detail. Summary helps move the story forward quickly. That way you, as the writer, can concentrate on creating scenes that show the most important moments in your plot.

Here, Charles Frazier in his novel *Cold Mountain* uses summary to show the distance Inman, the main male character, travels on his journey home.

> He calculated that his days of traveling had put little distance between himself and the hospital. His condition had required him to walk more slowly and to rest more often than he would have liked, and he had been able to cover only a few miles at a time, and even that slow pace had been at considerable cost.

Summary makes the time pass and history unfold quickly. Keep in mind, however, that summary, no matter how well written, ultimately distances the audience from the character and the immediacy of the story.

Even so, there are times when a scene just will not do.

This point was driven home to me during a plot workshop for memoir writers. I was explaining the importance of scene when one of the writers, a ninety-year-old woman, blurted out why her memoir does not work. "I've written it all in summary," she cried. She shook her head and looked away. Later, during her private consultation, her face crumbled and seemed to shapeshift into that of an agonized child. Though she was willing to rewrite her story to include scenes, I hesitated, wanting to caution her first. Summary allows you to purge yourself of your story by keeping the intimate and sometimes painful details at arm's length, I said as she dried her eyes. To write it in scenes, you'll have to relive it.

RESISTANCE TO THE PLOT PLANNER

Creative writing is an art. Many writers want to gain freedom from self-imposed limits. Too much freedom, however, often can lead you to wander forever without bringing a sense of coherence and closure to your story. Too much freedom works in direct opposition to your desired dream of creating a compelling story all the way to the end.

All stories begin with a character who wants something. They develop around dramatic action and end with the character transformed. Within the expansions and contractions of the Universal Story, the writer is free to do anything. But—and this is a very big *but*—only within the context of the structure of the Universal Story. Structure is where magic happens.

Remember, if you have determined your strength lies in writing dramatic action scenes, you will be more apt to embrace the plot planner strategies. If, on the other hand, you are a more character-driven writer, you likely will struggle with creating a plot planner. This is not to say you shouldn't make the attempt. Just be aware of any resistance that may crop up and adapt the plot planner in ways that more easily rely on your strengths.

If you are uncertain whether your story is primarily character-driven or action-driven or a combination of the two, study the scenes at the beginning and at the end of your story on the plot planner. An external, high-action, and dramatic climax close to the end of the story defines it as action-driven. If, at the climax, the character uses new skills, resources, and knowledge to face her greatest antagonist, something she was not able to do in the beginning of the story, your story likely is character-driven. If the character shows transformational behavior during a high-action climax, likely your story is a balance of the two plot structures.

The Major Elements of Any Plot

Plot is made up of three elements:

- Character emotional development
- Dramatic action
- Thematic significance

I said earlier that every character wants something. You (and your character) must decide what she is willing to give up to achieve her goal. This begins the character's emotional development plot.

The specific actions the character takes to realize her goal comprise the dramatic action plot.

Tie the character's private passion to a bigger, more transformative universal subject, and a thematic plot is launched. When the dramatic action changes the character over time, the story becomes thematically significant.

Think of the action, character, and thematic plot lines as parts of the whole. Then separate them and assign each plot a different color sticky note.

CHARACTER EMOTIONAL DEVELOPMENT

Stieg Larsson's *The Girl with the Dragon Tattoo* contains a plethora of plotlines. A mystery with a historical aspect intertwines with a political element and more. Of all the plotlines, what made me a fan of both the book and the movie is Lisbeth Salander's character emotional development and ultimate transformation.

I asked my book group, made up of women writers and one music aficionado, all of whom have read the book, what about this character draws us in so deeply and emotionally. Her impact on readers seems strange considering that she has such a flat emotional style and shares so little of herself with other characters. Her external landscape is essentially bare.

Here's what the women in my book group came up with in answer to why they find Lisbeth a compelling character:

- She is young and strange, possibly with symptoms of autism/ Aspergers.
- It's unusual to find a female protagonist who is so violent.
- Lisbeth doesn't belly up and lie down and take the abuse inflicted upon her by a flawed system and pathological men. She fights back and wins.
- She fights and wins not purely for her own interests. Unlike the woman they search for, Lisbeth does not run and hide and thus allow the perpetrator to destroy more women. She fights and wins to keep other women safe as well.
- She is smarter and wiser than the men in the story.
- When she is off the page, the story lags. As soon as she reappears, the story picks up momentum.
- She has been abandoned by everyone in her life.
- She starts out victimized, but is not a victim.
- A "misfit" wins and the "powerful" loses.
- Her visits to her mother show her humanity.

At the end of the beginning of *The Girl With the Dragon Tattoo*, Lisbeth is assigned a new guardian who seizes control of her finances and establishes that from now on when she needs money she must come to him for it. In that moment, Lisbeth loses control of her own affairs and is dependent on a man she does not trust. This scene plays out just twenty pages off the actual one-quarter page count. The crisis for her inner plot hits smack dab in the middle of the story, when Lisbeth's new guardian escalates his behavior from raping her to systematically and sadistically brutalizing her. Lisbeth understands no one is going to save her. Only she can save herself and other women like her.

In the crisis scene in which Lisbeth is brutalized by her guardian, Larsson both foreshadows what is to come (the main plot is concerned with tracking down a serial murderer who has been killing women for years) and also gives the character the insight needed for her ultimate transformation.

In the end, she outwits the serial killer by tapping into her true power. She shows her transformed self at the climax, thanks to every one of the dramatic action scenes she survived earlier in the story.

The thematic significance of this story shows in Lisbeth's character development plotline: one person, no matter how young and wounded, is able with cunning and patience to stop evil men from hurting women.

DRAMATIC ACTION

Throughout the story, the protagonist sets up goals for herself. These goals frame the dramatic action of the story and force the protagonist to move forward. The dramatic action is also called the front story.

A goal by itself does not create action that is dramatic. Obstacles that interfere with the protagonist's forward movement toward her goal do. That's especially true when the character stands to lose something significant if she's unable to reach her goal.

It's the same in real life. When your writing drifts and you get nowhere on your project, the problem and the solution revolve around one concrete and tangible element—every writer needs a goal that emboldens you to action.

PLOT WHISPER

Answer the following questions about your protagonist to help you create her goals:

- What does the protagonist most desire?
- What does she care about?
- What strongly motivates her?
- What is the character actively moving toward?
- What keeps her going, focused, committed when the going gets rough?
- What needs to be done, saved, protected, solved, fixed, achieved, figured out, helped that she and only she can do?
- What is her plan to accomplish that?

Goals give definition to your overall life and unfold moment-by-moment in your day. They give you two choices. Take steps toward your goal or shy away and drift.

One writer I counseled had the same dream for fifteen years. He yearned to hold in his hands a novel he had written. The problem was that the writer built up this dream so high that not just any novel would do. He must write the next Great American Novel.

Rather than face failure, the writer turned from the often lonely and tedious internal struggle of putting words on the page to the more tempting external road of worldly wealth and status. He quit writing.

Now, fifteen years later, he reclaimed his long-term goal of finishing by signing up for a series of ongoing plot consultations.

THEMATIC SIGNIFICANCE

Stories show a character changing, at the least, and transforming at the most profound. This potential for growth reflects meaning. Meaning reflects truth. The thematic significance of a story shows what all the words in each individual scene add up to. At its best, the significance of a story connects each individual reader and audience member to a moment of clarity about our shared relationship to a bigger picture through a wider complex of thoughts and relationships that exist outside the story.

THE WRITER'S WAY

Endure the fear of appearing foolish. The fear is justified. In the beginning, you may entertain grandiose goals. These will end up turning on you.

To achieve your goals, you must desperately want them, actively pursue them, and they must be within your power to achieve.

The more specific you are, the better your chances for success.

Similar to the protagonist's journey, you determine you own external goals while the Universal Story sets an invisible goal for you: to accept change. Fostering such an attitude foreshadows the changes necessary for the ultimate transformation to come.

What goals will you put everything else on the line for today?

The thematic significance of a story is a statement the story illustrates as truth. It can be plotted out scene by scene just as the dramatic action and the character emotional development are plotted out. In John Steinbeck's *East of Eden*, the protagonist, Cal, is the only character to change and transform. His emotional development from who he is at the beginning of the story to who he becomes at the end brings thematic significance to the idea the choices one makes, not one's blood, determine one's destiny.

In the beginning of your work, plot scenes introduce, define, and illustrate through dramatic action the individual elements of the story's thematic significance statement. These can include:

- Loss of family
- Rejection
- Abandonment
- Loyalty
- Responsibility
- Brothers, husband and wife, father and son, mother and son

Scenes in the first quarter of *East of Eden* show Caleb and his brother Aron fully at the mercy of others' choices and given names that seem to predict their destinies (names that reflect the biblical themes of the story). The end of the beginning scene shows Cal for the first time experiencing the consequences of an action he deliberately chose.

More sides of the themes are revealed in the middle of *East of Eden*. The exploration of secrets, right and wrong, good and evil, family bonds, shame and forgiveness, deepens the story and makes it richer and more complex. The theme of parental rejection and neglect that begins when Cal's mother shoots his father and leaves forever is repeated and intensified in the middle when Cal's father rejects him.

The end of *East of Eden* ties together all the themes introduced in the beginning and extended in the middle. Cal finally stops blaming his circumstances and begins taking responsibility for the choices he makes.

Communication at the thematic level is a complex composite of dynamic systems. One form of complex communication is through writing stories.

No matter how elusive, the deeper meaning of a story is rich and thick and holds magic. Writing sends you far into yourself. Along the journey, your themes, truths, and beliefs reveal themselves in surprising ways. Writing a story challenges you to figure out what matters most to you. Never strictly personal or for oneself, stories are written to be read. You strive to create a story big enough, important enough, and universal enough to warrant the reader's attention.

Themes bubble up out of the story itself. The thematic significance reflects the story's own view about life and how people behave. After a draft or two or three, you begin to understand the themes of your story and what they add up to in the end.

Explore and develop the broader meaning and message your story conveys about life or society and ultimately about human nature. The process of coaxing one thematic significance statement out of an entire project requires patience.

In the next chapter you will be given a chance to explore the themes of your story and begin to develop the thematic significance statement for your story.

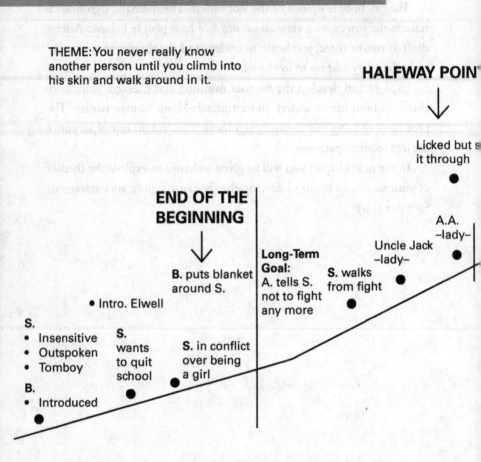

Figure 4.
Plot Planner for *To Kill a Mockingbird* by Harper Lee

THEME: You never really know another person until you climb into his skin and walk around in it.

HALFWAY POINT
↓

Licked but s
it through
●

END OF THE BEGINNING
↓

B. puts blanket around S.

A.A.
–lady–
●

Uncle Jack
–lady–
●

Long-Term Goal:
A. tells S. not to fight any more

● Intro. Elwell

S. walks from fight
●

S.
• Insensitive
• Outspoken
• Tomboy

S.
wants
to quit
school

S. in conflict over being a girl

B.
• Introduced

BEGINNING (¼)

MIDDLE (½)

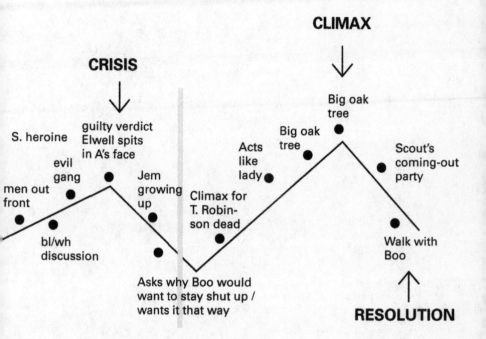

CLIMAX

CRISIS

Big oak
tree

S. heroine

guilty verdict
Elwell spits
in A's face

evil
gang

Jem
growing
up

men out
front

bl/wh
discussion

Big oak
tree

Acts
like
lady

Climax for
T. Robin-
son dead

Scout's
coming-out
party

Walk with
Boo

Asks why Boo would
want to stay shut up /
wants it that way

RESOLUTION

END (¼)

B = Boo
A = Atticus
S = Scout
AA = Aunt Alexandra

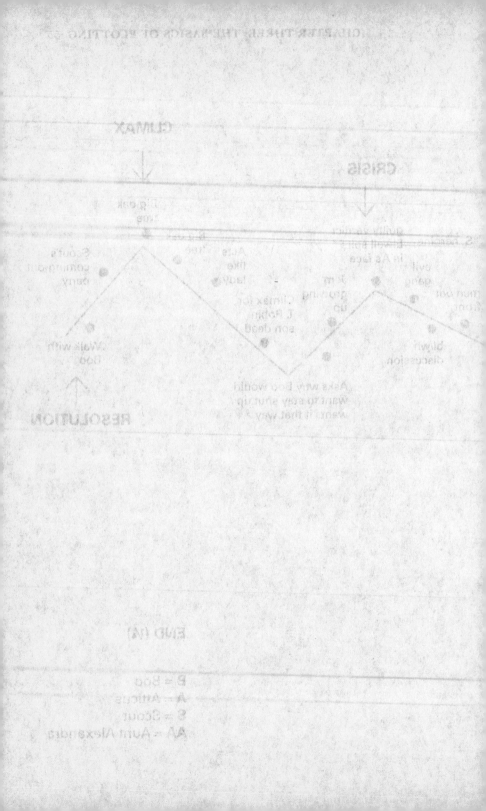

CHAPTER FOUR
DEVELOPING THEMES

To produce a mighty book you must choose a mighty theme.

—Herman Melville

Every story communicates its own unique pattern of themes and ideas: betrayal, loyalty, family, abuse, isolation, romance, failure, injustice, unfairness, poverty, good versus evil, forgiveness, and love.

Right-Brain and Left-Brain Thematic Significance

We have touched on the two sides of the interconnected brain. In discussing theme:

- The right hemisphere has the ability to evaluate communication in relationship to the bigger picture.
- The left hemisphere tends to interpret things literally.

When it comes to tapping into a story's deeper meaning, a whole brain approach is best, one in which all knowledge is intimately linked.

If you tend to interpret things literally and have difficulty grasping the thematic significance of your story, talk to writers who are less linear, organized, and literal than you are. Big-picture writers may see the deeper meaning of your story long before you do. By the same token, a right-brained writer benefits from learning what her left-brained, more literal counterpart has to say about her abstract story.

A Third Type of Writer

Beyond the two types of writers we have discussed is a third type, one who is more rare than the other two. Rather than approach a story from the dramatic action first or from developing the character, this writer comes at writing a story first from its thematic significance.

During a consultation several years ago I encountered such a writer. Not only did she excel at thematic significance, she drowned in it. She filled out a character emotional development plot profile for her protagonist (a female) that was full of abstract concepts. Her chief character wanted to right the wrongs done to the blind, especially by the medical profession. But rather than giving the protagonist a concrete, measurable, and attainable goal such as drafting new legislation, the writer created pages of dialogue and summary. When her characters acted, their actions were usually devoid of emotional clues. The writer grew up as a sighted child with a mother, father, sister, grandparents, and a community who were all blind; this unique perspective gave her a huge advantage in writing this story. But she over-focused on a heavy thematic message and was unable to write in moment-by-moment scenes.

Although it may be tempting to tell your readers about your strongly held beliefs, criticisms, and judgments, such thematic micro-focus can quickly turn into "information dumping." Piling on large quantities of information creates distance between you and the reader. Even when the information is thematically rich, unless it's presented elegantly and meaningfully through the characters' actions, you'll alienate the average reader.

Rather than write the dramatic action of the journey the protagonist takes and her ultimate transformation, writers sometimes lecture and argue. When they do create dramatic action and reveal a glimmer of the character's emotional reaction through her actions, their own emotions twist her out of the here-and-now of the story.

THE WRITER'S WAY

The Universal Story connects us energetically to everything else here on earth and galactically. Like a ripple on a lake, each thought, emotion, and story blends into all other thoughts, emotions, and stories.

Such a shift in perception moves a single, individual entity into a sense of interconnectedness. No longer isolated and alone, we are as big as the universe and linked to the energy flow of all that is.

Themes underlie the surface attitudes and actions of the characters in your story. To identify the deeper meaning of your story, you must know yourself and your story very well. When it comes to understanding the thematic significance of your story, be patient and allow the deeper meaning of your story to evolve naturally from the story itself. Every day, stand back from your plot planner and concentrate on the whole story.

A heavy mantle of responsibility often drives theme-centric writers to deliver an indignant message. The terror of not being capable of pulling off the feat crushes them. Even deeper, their fear of facing their own buried emotions causes them to doubt their abilities. Fear stalls, cripples, and damages the writing process more than any lack of actual writing ability.

How to Identify and Plot Thematic Elements

You have written some fine prose. You feel good about your characters. The exotic world is unique and the dramatic action exciting. Now it is time to explore what your story is saying.

The Pulitzer Prize–winning novel *The Grapes of Wrath* by John Steinbeck deals with the injustices inflicted upon poor people in the Great Depression of the thirties during the Dust Bowl migration. Especially, it relates how one Oklahoma farm family, the Joads, driven from their homestead, travel west to the promised land of California. The story touches on trials and violence, hunger and fear, the collision between the Haves and the Have-Nots, and the tragic but ultimate insistence on human dignity.

Every one of the words in the above description of the novel is a theme: injustice, poverty, migration, depression, journey, violence, hunger, fear, collision, and human dignity.

What separates great books from good books is the degree to which an author is able to voice something only she and her unique truth can tell. The deeper meaning of your story and your life fills you with energy to write and live a more fulfilled life. The thematic significance statement reflects the truth of your story. This is not necessarily a universal truth or truth for all time, but it is true for your story.

The themes in your story must be worthy enough for you to give up hours of your life to write about them, for the character to go through the struggle of a journey, and for the reader to spend hours reading your story. Do not despair if such thematic significance does not appear immediately. It will.

Stories with themes of the earth and nature, interdependence, and empathy vibrate differently than do themes of war and death, isolation, and fear. The more you home in on the deeper meaning of your story and the big problem that needs to be solved in your protagonist's life, the more focused the scenes will be and the richer their presentation.

Identify Your Story's General Themes

Many writers scoot as far away as possible from the thematic significance of their stories. I believe, instead, that you should dive right in. That is what the search for meaning feels like—diving into a cool, dark, mysterious pool of water.

Draw a large oval on an oversized piece of paper. Create smaller circles that connect to and radiate out from the oval. For now, leave the oval blank.

Fill in the smaller "bubbles" with themes in your story. You may find yourself dabbling with themes of fairness, rivalry, blame, regret, destruction, isolation, nature versus nurture, or something else entirely. Where one theme, such as justice, relates to other themes, such as corruption, greed, injustice, and rebellion, connect the circles to each other.

The more you delve into theme, the more you'll notice themes all around you. Add new bubbles as new themes crop up.

When you come up with a thematic significance statement, even if it does not feel exactly right or ring 100 percent true, print the sentence in pencil in the large, center oval. With the statement in place, review the theme bubbles you created. Does the statement in the center oval include the major themes from the bubbles? If not, can you adapt the sentence to consist of more? Or, adapt the themes in the bubbles so they more closely fit your overall theme?

Some themes drop off after one or two scenes. Cross off any that are no longer relevant. Others show up in one form or another consistently in most scenes. Ask yourself what those themes mean to you. What beliefs do you carry about those ideas? Are they consistent with what is expressed in your story? Draw more theme circles as they come to you. Highlight any that feel true. A pattern begins to emerge.

When you first plan your plot, your themes are likely sketchy with gaps and dead ends. These gaps will smooth over and fill in as you better understand what your story is about and you know your characters better.

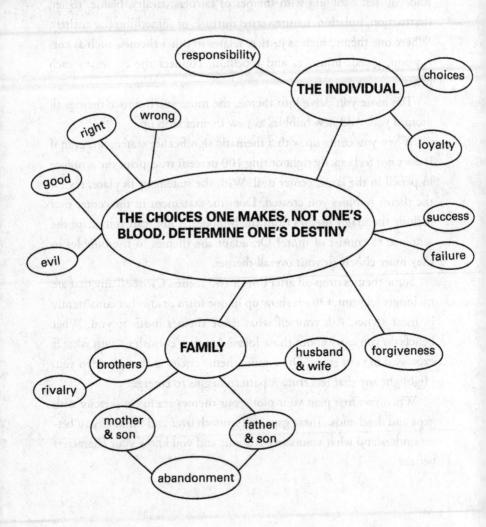

Figure 5.
Thematic Significance Bubble Template for *East of Eden*
by John Steinbeck

PLOT WHISPER

Figure out your obsession. Say, for instance, you are obsessed with finding out who you really are, your own unique identity. Generate scenes with that in mind—the character's interaction with others, trying to figure out her place in the world. This is a universal theme for all of us.

As you write, try to make a significant thematic statement as an action point: how does one figure out her place in the world? Through trial and error? Okay. Put the two ideas together to create a broad thematic significance statement: Finding one's place in the world requires trial and error. Now, make the broad thematic significance statement relevant to your individual story. Tack on a phrase at the beginning or the end that qualifies, limits, or modifies the broader thematic significance as it applies to what happens in your story. Describe and provide a more accurate meaning for how your book satisfies the requirements of the thematic significance statement. Finding one's place in the world takes trial and error and in the end brings . . . what? What does all the dramatic action in all the scenes illustrate? What does the character's transformation symbolize about where one belongs and about suffering trials and errors? There are as many ways to end that statement as there are writers and stories: . . . and in the end brings tragedy, fulfillment, satisfaction, power, corruption, destroys the old and creates the new.

The love of a girl for a boy and overcoming great odds is the first part of a thematic significance statement. Now, give relevance to that beginning by condensing the overall meaning of your story into one statement that relates to the broad thematic significance of your specific story. Because a girl loves a boy, she is able to overcome great odds, to protect herself, and in the process to protect other women, too.

- How is meaning activated in your story?
- What do all the scenes add up to?
- What does that mean?
- Why is that important?
- Write that as one sentence.

Creating Energetic Markers

The act of creating something from nothing connects us to the Universal Story. Four scenes or moments in the Universal Story carry energetic surges that are powerful enough to turn the dramatic action of the story in a new direction, create a whole new level of intensity in the story, and contribute to its thematic significance. Whenever possible, strive to identify these four energetic markers early in the writing process.

The energy of the Universal Story rises and falls at predetermined moments, marking the passage from birth to growth to death and rebirth. Every story has its own energy that operates within the universal pattern and contributes to the whole. The energetic markers guide you where and when to direct the flow of your scenes and how to encourage the energy to crest and fall for the greatest emotional impact. Knowledge of energetic markers in stories allows you to shape your story in the most compelling manner for the reader.

The scenes in the beginning quarter of the story have less conflict, tension, and suspense than do the scenes that come in the final quarter of the story. Think of your story as energy that rises to each of the energetic markers and falls after each of those turning points, only to rise again even higher at the next major scene.

Like signposts, energetic markers identify four major turning points in every story. Each energetic marker defines the dramatic action, characters, and thematic significance plot elements as your story energy expands and recedes.

FIRST ENERGETIC MARKER: END OF THE BEGINNING

By the end of the beginning, the protagonist has appeared in varying situations. Her emotions have been introduced by showing the reader how she usually responds to the action around her.

PLOT WHISPER

On a colored sticky note, write a scene title for the end-of-the-beginning scene for your story. Place the note above the first high point on the plot planner you drew and hung on the wall, about one-quarter from where the line begins on the left.

Now ask yourself what the main elements in that scene title convey. Something mostly about the character? Mostly about the action? Mostly the theme? A combination of the three?

Your answer will probably indicate whether you're a left-brained or right-brained writer, or if you take a more balanced approach.

Do not confuse introduction with passivity. The opening of the story introduces the core conflict of the story, which becomes the basis of the dramatic action—the protagonist wants something she thinks she cannot have. Dramatic action calls for conflict, tension, suspense, and/or curiosity. The beginning introduces the reader to every thematic element through mood, tone, voice, word choices, metaphors and similes, and authentic details. The savvy reader knows on some level these are important to the overall story. By the end of the first quarter of the story, the audience and readers are grounded in the here-and-now of the story world and all the elements of the climax have been foreshadowed. Usually, the reader senses a change coming as the energy of the story builds to the official close of the beginning, but not always.

Alexandra Fuller closes in on the quarter mark of her memoir, *Don't Let's Go to the Dogs Tonight*, with nary a hint of the first energetic marker.

As the energy continues to stay flat, the reader, unwittingly, begins to feel a bit antsy. Then . . . BAM! The end of the beginning scene hits. Completely unprepared for the turning point in the story that happens exactly one-quarter of the way into the memoir, the reader is startled, sits up, and takes notice.

THE END OF THE BEGINNING THRESHOLD MOMENT

Between leaving the beginning quarter of your story and formally entering the middle, the protagonist first finds herself at a threshold. At this pivotal moment, all choices for the protagonist narrow down to just two:

1. Fade out and die
2. Move forward into the unknown

Thresholds symbolize the moment after one phase of the Universal Story ends and just before the next phase begins. Every moment turns on a threshold decision between old and new. All beings on earth cross this line at predetermined stages—from seed to sapling to tree, caterpillar to chrysalis to butterfly. Each year, one season comes and then turns into another. Each time between what was and what will be is a gap, a threshold.

A threshold signals a transition. Cross this line and you cross into the unknown. A thousand tiny butterfly wings flutter in your stomach. Your throat turns dry. Your body senses a change is coming before your conscious mind does. In that moment, you are suspended between what has always been and what is coming next. Energy rushes up your spine.

Thresholds in stories are especially effective as the character turns away from the beginning of the story and before she steps into the middle.

As the first quarter of a story winds to a close, a scene or event symbolizes the end of what is. The protagonist separates from all that is familiar. Her sense of self is shaken. Her attachment to learned attitudes and behavior is severed. The energy surges and the story turns in a new direction, launching the protagonist into the actual story world itself with a goal that takes on greater meaning.

In the book *Harry Potter and the Sorcerer's Stone* by J. K. Rowling, when Harry leaves his evil relatives for the magical school Hogwarts, his old life ends and his new life as a wizard in training begins. In *The Grapes of Wrath* when the Joad family drives off toward California with all their worldly possessions strapped to their truck, their old life ends and their new life begins. In *Watership Down* by Richard Adams, when Hazel and his friends leave behind their old warren and set out to find the perfect environment and create a warren of their own, their lives change forever. In all these cases, the threshold marks the point at which the real adventure begins.

If you have not identified this moment in your project, look at the scenes somewhere around the first quarter of the book. You are looking for a moment that signifies the end of the way things have always been, a scene that launches the protagonist into the actual story world, and signifies that there is no turning back. When you find the scene that serves this purpose, rewrite it with the significance it deserves. Be sure to include details that stimulate all five senses: hearing, seeing, touching, smelling, and tasting. Make sure the scene does not arrive too far beyond one quarter of the way into the project or you may find your readers' or viewers' interest waning.

SECOND ENERGETIC MARKER: HALFWAY POINT

The second turning point, coming halfway through the story, forces the protagonist to willingly and consciously commit to the journey. After recommitting to her goal(s) at the halfway point of the Universal Story, or for the reluctant hero committing for the first time, the protagonist feels the energy in her life turn and rise in significance. This energetic surge is a warning to the reader. Wake up. Be alert. A crisis is coming.

PLOT WHISPER

Locate your recommitment scene somewhere around the halfway mark of your story. If you do not find one, perhaps you have misidentified the energy of the scenes. Look instead at what you believe is the crisis scene, usually set at the three-quarter mark. Often that scene in fact is the recommitment scene and fits at the halfway point, perfectly.

Compare the energetic difference between the recommitment scene at the halfway mark and what is needed at the true crisis, the breakdown scene. Often what writers believe is the crisis does not have enough energy to fulfill the elements needed at the crisis.

If the energy of what you wrote as a crisis scene is not intense enough to qualify for the spot, see if the scene better fits the recommitment scene.

Wherever you find the recommitment scene, create a title that clearly identifies the scene. For now, simply notice if the title you write down is character-driven, action-driven, thematically driven, or a combination of the three. Affix a sticky note with the scene title above the line at the midpoint of the plot planner.

Stand back from the plot planner. View the end-of-the-beginning scene and the halfway-point scene in relationship to each other.

THIRD ENERGETIC MARKER: THE CRISIS

At nearly three-quarters of the way through the story, the energy rises to a breaking point. The third energetic marker is the crisis, the greatest struggle of the entire story so far.

After surviving this ordeal toward the end of the middle of the story, the protagonist transmutes. But before the protagonist can transform, her old persona must, effectively, die. This is the role of the crisis.

Each scene in the middle portion of your story serves to march the protagonist step-by-step to the crisis. The energy builds until the volcano erupts, or the river overflows.

The protagonist believes she is moving nearer and nearer to her long-term goal and consequent success. When the crisis hits, she is traumatized. The reader, however, has experienced the steady incline in the story's energy and feels the inevitability of this shocker from the linkage between each scene and from each thematic detail.

PLOT WHISPER

Finding the exact right placement for your scenes to create the highest energetic and thematic intensity often proves difficult. A writer in one of my workshops placed a high emotional impact scene in the beginning, which her critique group criticized as ineffective. In reaction to the feedback, the writer cut the scene all together. However, when that same scene was used as the crisis, the scene worked wonderfully on a multitude of levels. A natural disaster filled with conflict, tension, and suspense turned out to be the perfect metaphor for the swirling emotions the protagonist felt in the dark night of her soul.

Usually all the elements are always right there in front of you. Your work as a writer is to craft the scenes into a well-plotted story.

Once you locate the crisis scene, create a title that best encapsulates it and put the sticky note above the peak on the plot planner around the three-quarter mark. Again, for now, simply note which plot element(s) in the scene (action, character, theme) the title represents.

FOURTH ENERGETIC MARKER: THE CLIMAX

The fourth energetic marker holds the greatest intensity and highest drama in the entire story. It is called the climax.

PLOT WHISPER

The climax scene often poses the greatest difficulty for writers. Even after you've faced your own personal demons and written the crisis that sends the protagonist to her death — metaphorically speaking, of course — you find yourself hitting a wall at the base of Climax Mountain. You lose energy for your story. You may find yourself feeling wary and numb over the scenes still left to write.

A writer who has not experienced a transformation in her own life often cannot see, feel, touch, smell, and hear the scene depicting such a moment for the protagonist.

Encourage the protagonist to do what she needs to do. For now, write action only. Stop trying to get in the character's head. Reveal the protagonist through her actions as the powerhouse she can and must be.

When you feel like you have a climax scene, stand back and compare the scenes at each of the four energetic markers. Ask yourself if the scenes qualify energetically for each spot. Yes? Then the structure of your story is now in place.

These four energetic markers appear in romance novels, screenplays, mysteries, young adult, memoirs, middle grade, and yes, even picture books. These four energetically charged scenes or events bring meaning to your story.

At the climax of the story, all the forces of the story come together for the final clash in which the protagonist directly conflicts with her major antagonist(s). Just when it looks as if all is permanently lost for the protagonist, she displays a rediscovered or refined awareness, skill, and/or knowledge. The climax is the crowning moment of the entire story, when the thematic significance of your story becomes clear to the reader.

The action by the protagonist answers the dramatic question posed at the beginning of the story: Will she or won't she be victorious? At the climax, all major conflicts are resolved. The energy of the entire story crescendos at the climax and immediately is defused.

THE WRITER'S WAY

Date a new entry in your journal and write your impressions of the four scenes on your plot planner. Concentrate on how you feel energetically now that you have started plotting. How is your energy level affected by what you see on the plot planner?

- Does what you see excite you about writing the story in front of you?
- Are you calmly confident and ready to move forward?
- Do you shake your head at what you see on your plot planner?
- Does what you see there deflate or build your energy?

Write the words you say to yourself and how those words affect you emotionally and energetically. Be honest about how you encourage, congratulate, or tear yourself down. How you treat yourself now is an introduction to how you likely will treat yourself throughout the writing of the story. The process of writing a story from beginning to end is filled with challenges. Develop an awareness of your relationship to yourself as a writer. Explore ways to enliven your energy for writing. Trust the process and believe in the possibility of transformation.

PART TWO

CREATE THE CHARACTERS AND SETTING: WHO'S PART OF THIS WORLD AND WHY?

CHAPTER FIVE

WHO INHABITS THE PLOT?

When writing a novel, a writer should create living people.

—Ernest Hemingway

Now that we've established the general ebb and flow of energy in the plot structure, it's time to turn our attention to the issue of *characters*. Of course, I've talked about this a bit already. But we need to place those characters in the context of the plot's structure and see what function each one performs in moving the Universal Story forward to its crisis and eventually its climax.

The Protagonist

The protagonist of a story is the character most changed by the dramatic action. All other characters and the setting(s), too, influence the protagonist's journey toward her goal directly, indirectly, or thematically. The growth and transformation of the protagonist is the line that runs through the entire plot.

PLOT WHISPER

Cut out of a magazine a picture that represents your protagonist, or use a photo of someone you know who embodies the strengths and flaws you envision for your protagonist. Or, choose an actor you can visualize playing the role of the protagonist. Affix this visual representation of your main character to your plot planner to help stimulate ideas.

THE PROTAGONIST'S GOAL

Whether they say it in so many words, writers who develop a protagonist with clearly defined goals are more apt to stay focused. Ultimately, this clarity translates to the reader. A reader who knows what motivates the main character is able to closely connect and stay involved with the protagonist, and to calculate the progress the main character makes, or doesn't. The reader roots for her when she's successful and mourns when she is confronted with failure.

The ability to create tangible and concrete goals appropriate to the protagonist is critical to stories. Specific and concrete long-term goals create a dramatic question: Will she or won't she achieve her goal?

PLOT WHISPER

In this chapter, you will be given a Character Emotional Development Plot Profile to fill out for your protagonist and any other major characters. This task is helpful for two reasons.

1. Your answers create your story's dramatic action plot and the characters' emotional development plots.
2. Your answers reveal, as a sort of self-diagnostic exercise, whether you are classically left- or right-brained.

If you have little trouble filling out the first three items that revolve around concrete goal setting, but you struggle with the last seven items, chances are you are a left-brained writer.

If you can easily fill out the last seven items identifying character traits, but you leave blank the goal-setting queries, you likely display classic strengths and weaknesses of a right-brained writer.

Fill out all ten items with ease and you probably write holistically, with strengths balanced on both sides.

BEGINNING GOALS

The establishment of the first goal at the beginning of the story launches the dramatic action plot. The other goal settings keep the energy of the dramatic action plot moving higher and faster. Each time you make your protagonist's goal known to the audience the energy swells.

Often, the protagonist's long-term goal is implied at the beginning of stories rather than fixed. Dramatic action causes the protagonist to react, which, in turn, forms her first stated or overt goal. Characters need definable action through which to express their emotions.

For example: Sixteen-year-old Juno, in the Oscar-winning best original screenplay *Juno* by Diablo Cody, begins the story with a goal of assessing if she truly is pregnant. Beneath her tough, no-nonsense exterior, Juno reveals herself as a teenager trying to figure out where she fits in life. The concrete nature of the goal—finding out if she is pregnant or not—grounds the reader. The universality of her implied long-term, abstract goal of figuring out her life excites hope in the audience that this movie will help inform their own life decisions.

The long-term goal often changes at the first energetic marker. An event or action signals the end of the beginning and a moment of no return, the end of what has always been. This event catapults the main character into the heart of the story world itself. Usually, the character enters the middle of the story with a revised goal.

At the one-quarter mark of the screenplay, Juno tells her boyfriend she is pregnant. The need to make choices pushes her into the reality of being a pregnant teen. Even in this new world, she remains true to her earlier goal of trying to figure out how she fits into life. But now the goal has changed because the world into which she needs to integrate is different—it's the adult world rather than that of a teenager. Her goal now triggers in the audience their own judgments of what a teen in her position "should" do.

Obstacles and antagonists in the middle of the story force the protagonist to re-evaluate and redefine her goals. The scene that marks the second energetic marker at the halfway point in the story shows the protagonist recommitting to her goal or shifting that commitment to a new goal.

Juno's first goal of getting an abortion fails. Next she finds a couple willing to adopt the baby after it is born. Exactly halfway through the screenplay, Juno tells the wife that she is "104 percent" sure she is going to go ahead with the adoption plans they have made.

At the third energetic marker toward the end of the middle, the protagonist's goal changes again. The energy at the crisis is intense enough to knock the protagonist to her knees. She rises from the ashes of her old self with a shift in her external goals to reflect symbolically or thematically who she is now becoming.

Three-quarters of the way through the screenplay *Juno*, the husband of the couple planning to adopt Juno's unborn baby tells the pregnant teenager that he no longer loves his wife and intends to get a divorce. Juno panics when she understands that the perfect family she has planned for her baby is not so perfect after all. Based on her backstory, Juno has constructed a picture in her mind of the perfect family for her unborn child, which includes a mother and a father. When that perfection for her baby shatters, Juno shatters, too. The crisis causes her to redefine her idea of a perfect family, which takes her one step nearer to forgiveness and accomplishing an unconscious goal of healing the wound caused years earlier in her backstory when her mother left her. She revises her earlier goal of finding a mother and father for her baby and moves forward into the end of the story with a new goal. She keeps this goal a secret until after the climax of the story and reveals it in her note to the single adoptive mother: "If you're still in, I'm still in—Juno."

We can plot Juno's changes on a Character Emotional Development Profile.

Character Emotional Development Profile

Title: *Juno*

Character's name: *Juno*

1. What is the protagonist's goal?

   Beginning of the Story: *Find out if she is pregnant*

   Middle of the Story: *Determine what to do now that she knows she is pregnant*

   End of the Story: *Tell Bleeker how she feels about him*

2. What obstacles interfere with her success?

   Beginning of the Story: *Her refusal to accept she is pregnant*

   Middle of the Story: *Confusion over abortion, inability to find the perfect family*

   End of the Story: *Disbelief in the possibility of two people remaining in love together*

3. What does she stand to lose if not successful?

   Beginning of the Story: *Her youthful exuberance*

   Middle of the Story: *All control over her life and future*

   End of the Story: *The best friend she's ever had and his unconditional love that lets shine her confident, nonchalant, and effortless attitude*

Figure 6. Character Emotional Development Profile for *Juno* by Diablo Cody

The Protagonist's Flaw

A core plot of your story revolves around your protagonist's inner development. To satisfy this inner plot, the protagonist must undergo a deep and fulfilling transformation. Often you can accomplish this by creating a flawed character. Eventually, she will have to face that flaw and overcome it in order to achieve her ultimate goal.

At the beginning of *To Kill a Mockingbird*, Scout is insensitive to others. Harper Lee shows Scout's lack of empathy in the early scene in which Scout and her brother Jem meet Dill, a secondary character who represents the "romance" plot of the novel.

Scout's lack of emotional development at the beginning of the book results in large part from her age as well as the early death of her mother. You must recognize that the flaws with which you imbue your character do not come out of the blue. As with Scout's, they usually originate in reaction to something in the character's backstory.

Scout persists in asking Dill about his father even though Dill clearly has chosen not to mention him. Dill becomes flustered by Scout's lack of tact when she refuses to accept his answer of not having one and presses him further. He outright blushes when she states the obvious: "if he's not dead, you've got one, haven't you?" Even then, Scout would have persisted with her questioning if Jem hadn't hushed her. Later that summer, Scout shows no concern for her neighbor Boo's feelings when she demonstrates her acceptance without question that he is a malevolent phantom.

After the crisis, Scout begins to overcome her flaw of insensitivity when she wonders for the first time why Boo stays shut up in his house and why he wants it that way. At the end of the book, having been transformed by her experiences, Scout shows empathy through a series of emotionally and thematically rich actions in the final two chapters of the novel.

Scout wonders why Atticus invites the sheriff and Boo to the front door instead of the living room and then understands that the living room lights are awfully bright. She leads Boo to the chair on the porch in the deep shadows, showing her newfound sensitivity. She knows without being told that Boo will feel more comfortable in the dark. She turns downright tenderhearted when she sits down beside him. After she has him escort her to his home and he disappears inside, she stands on his front porch and sees the world as he has always seen it. In that moment she shows the full integration of the story's thematic significance: you never really know a man until you stand in his shoes and walk around in them. "Just standing on the Radley porch was enough."

In *Juno*, the protagonist's flaw is her cavalier behavior. Yes, this can-do kid makes great grades, has friends, and is kind and intelligent. But she often acts tough to hide an emotional void. Quickly we learn that her no-nonsense exterior is a breastplate protecting a tender heart (Juno's mother left her when she was just a child). Juno's prickly exterior also keeps people at arm's length, a feature that ultimately interferes with her attempts to find her place in the world and satisfy her long-term goal.

Examples of Character Flaws

- Always the victim and unable to take responsibility for actions
- Control freak
- Argumentative and short-tempered
- Liar and a cheat
- Stubborn
- Always has to be right
- Perfectionist
- Procrastinator
- Sits in judgment

Creating a Character Emotional Development Plot Profile

Assess who your protagonist is at the beginning of the story and what she wants. This is "baseline data." It prepares you to create dramatic action scenes. It ensures the reader is clear from the beginning of the book about who the protagonist is and what she wants. By the end of the story, the protagonist is changed and transformed. To evaluate the extent of that change later, record where the character is now.

Later in this chapter I'll present what I call the Character Emotional Development Plot Profile. The prompts on this ten-point plot questionnaire reveal the split in stories between character emotional development and dramatic action.

Dramatic Action Goals

The first three items on the character profile establish the dramatic action plot. In order to achieve her long-term goal, the protagonist must act and meet antagonists head-on. This is what creates the drama of the plot.

These first three major items on the profile have to do with goal setting:

1. Goals provide motivation.
2. Obstacles create tension.
3. Potential loss promises transformation.

MOTIVATION

The character's overall goal is attainable. The character may need help, but he or she is the initiator of the ultimate action that creates the fulfillment of the goal at the climax of the story. This is true whether you're writing for children, young adults, or adult readers. The child or teen protagonist of a story may need the help of a parent or the police or a teacher, but she will initiate the action and/or call for help.

In the very first illustration of the fifty-year-old classic picture book *Where the Wild Things Are* by Maurice Sendak, Max, the protagonist, is hammering a nail in the living room wall and chasing the dog—actions that convey his desire to be a wild thing.

An engaging character with a long-term and worthy goal is not enough. To create excitement, something must impede the main character from moving forward. Antagonists—whether human or non-human, concrete or abstract—prevent the protagonist from achieving his goal and create conflict, tension, suspense, and curiosity.

OBSTACLES

For action-driven stories such as thrillers, mysteries, and suspense, the antagonist(s) standing in the way of the protagonist may be overt. The villain may have goals that are in direct opposition to those of the main character. For character-driven fiction, the antagonist(s) may be internal: flaws, fears, and prejudices. In this case, the character's inner demons interfere with her progress. A balanced story takes advantage of both external and internal antagonists. External antagonists challenge her throughout the story and especially in the middle. They know how to push her, to ignite her flaws, to create gaps of imbalance, and become what she must overcome for ultimate success.

In *Where the Wild Things Are*, Max's mother interferes with Max's goal of being a wild thing and thus serves as an antagonist.

POTENTIAL LOSS

This determines what motivates the protagonist to keep striving for her goals even in the face of tremendous odds. The greater the risk, the more exciting the story.

The protagonist who chooses to stay focused and committed to the achievement of her long-term goal, even in the face of enormous antagonists, is often motivated by:

- Vengeance
- Love or hate
- A promise
- Rebellion
- Betrayal
- Persecution
- Self-sacrifice
- Survival
- Rivalry

- Ambition
- Grief and loss

In *Where the Wild Things Are* Max resists his mother's interference and loses his dinner.

PLOT WHISPER

Fill in the goal items on the Character Emotional Development Profile with what you know so far about the protagonist of your story. Leave blank what eludes you. (The blanks you leave on the character profile for your protagonist say as much about you as a writer as what you fill in. Refer to Chapter One for more information about the two types of writers. Then look back at what you've filled in on the profile. Does this confirm that you're a left-brained or a right-brained writer?)

Return to your plot planner. Choose a specific color to signify the dramatic action plot and write down the protagonist's goal on a colored sticky note. Stick that note at the far left and very beginning of your plot planner. This sticky note signifies the beginning of the dramatic action plot.

Add the same color sticky note at each of the first three energetic markers in your story. These convey how the protagonist's goals shift as the energy of the dramatic action swirls one-quarter of the way through your story, then again in the middle, and after three-quarters of the way to the end of your story. Note the major obstacles that interfere with the protagonist's success and the reasons she continues on her quest, even in the face of apparent disaster.

Character Emotional Development Traits

The final seven items on the Character Emotional Development Profile will help you to create a character emotional development arc.

FLAW

The main character's flaw sets up the overall character arc and points to the potential for growth or transformation. Her flaw interferes with achieving her goal.

Max's flaw in *Where the Wild Things Are* is his wild activity.

STRENGTH

Throughout the story, the protagonist faces many obstacles. Her strength contributes to the forward movement of the story, because every time she is knocked down, she has the strength to get back up and continue toward her goal.

Max's strength in *Where the Wild Things Are* is his imagination.

LOVE

A character capable of loving something or someone is likeable in the eyes of the reader.

In *Where the Wild Things Are*, Max loves his mother.

HATE

Hate is an intense emotion and provides character complexity.

In *Where the Wild Things Are*, Max hates being told what to do.

FEARS

A character who fears something is vulnerable. A fear is something that has not happened yet, and a character's fear reveals what part of her is missing. What the protagonist fears most is precisely what she must face in order to transform and restore a sense of balance in her life.

In *Where the Wild Things Are*, Max fears loneliness.

DREAMS

Dreams or desires add yet another layer to a story. Dreams generally rely on the help of others or a bit of magic and, thus, create an added twist at the end of the story.

In *Where the Wild Things Are*, Max dreams of becoming king of the wild things.

SECRETS

Not all characters have secrets, or they may not all reveal their secrets. If a secret comes to you, write it down. A secret often provides a plot twist in the story.

In *Where the Wild Things Are*, Max's secret is his love for his mother.

PLOT WHISPER

Fill in the character traits on the Character Emotional Development Profile, describing what you know so far about the protagonist of your story. Leave blank what eludes you. (Again, the blanks you leave on the character profile for your protagonist say as much about you as a writer as what you fill in. Refer to Chapter One for more information about the two types of writers.)

Return to your plot planner. Using the same color of sticky note that you chose to signify the character emotional development plot, write down the protagonist's flaw. Stick that note at the far left and very beginning of your plot planner above the sticky note for the character's goal and dramatic action plot. This new sticky note signifies the beginning of the character emotional development plot.

Re-evaluate the character emotional development sticky notes at each of the first three energetic markers in your story. Do they convey how the protagonist's flaw shifts as the energy of the dramatic action rises one-quarter of the way through your story, then deepens in the middle, and is ripped away after three-quarters of the way to the end of your story? Add notes to reflect the protagonist's emotional developmental changes and how her flaw interferes with success on her quest.

CHARACTER EMOTIONAL DEVELOPMENT PROFILE

Fill out the following profile for your protagonist and all major characters.

Character's name:

Dramatic Action Plotline

1. Overall story goal:
2. What stands in her/his way?
3. What does s/he stand to lose?

Character Emotional Development Plotline

1. Flaw(s):
2. Strength(s):
3. Hate(s):
4. Love(s):
5. Fear(s):
6. Dream(s):
7. Secret(s):

Figure 7. Character Emotional Development Plot Profile

How to Use a Character Flaw

A character flaw is a coping mechanism that arises from the loss of an original state of perfection that occurred in the character's backstory. Her flaw is designed to compensate for a perceived vulnerability, sense of insecurity, and feeling threatened. No matter how confident, every major character demonstrates lessons learned from the wound inflicted in her backstory that now is lodged in her core belief system.

IN THE BEGINNING

The beginning of your story establishes who the character is, flaws and all. Your readers can look back to this portrait and compare it to who she becomes as she undergoes a transformation after the crisis. The portrait also foreshadows who she will be at the climax.

In one of my workshops, I reviewed a writer's historical novel that took place in Napa Valley on the family vineyard. Her character profile was missing a flaw for the protagonist even after she had written several drafts of the story.

The writer ran through the energetic markers on her plot planner. As she reread what she had written on the character emotional development sticky note at the third energetic marker—a scene in which the protagonist was unable to stand up for himself when it most counted (character emotional development crisis)—the writer knew she had found the protagonist's flaw.

Realizing that the protagonist's passivity was a character flaw, the writer went about developing this trait throughout the story. In so doing, she made every scene before the crisis reflect more honestly and dramatically a deeper understanding of the protagonist.

Plagued with doubts about himself, the protagonist wilted when confronted by others. He gave in to his younger brother's wishes, even for things he really wanted. Because he couldn't stand up for himself, he never got what he desired. This trait, which the writer showed early in the story, made for a more dramatic character transformation in the end. The protagonist was content to shrink into second position because he did not have the sort of power or personality for a leadership position, until . . . his mother died (dramatic action crisis). With the loss of his only ally, he was on his own. To keep his promise and run things as she left them he had to transform and to fight.

IN THE MIDDLE

A character flaw introduced in the beginning quarter of the story deepens as the energy of the story expands in the middle half. More and more often the protagonist trips up. Finally, she no longer can deny her own part in her failure. This newfound awareness brings about her ultimate transformation in the last quarter of the story.

At the beginning of *The Girl With the Dragon Tattoo*, the reader learns that as a result of trauma suffered as a child, Lisbeth has forgotten how to love. A warrior out to protect her heart at all costs, she holds herself separate from others, especially men. In the middle of the story, the more she interacts with Mikael Blomkvist, the more she learns about herself. When he is threatened at the dramatic action crisis, her heart, now cracked open, can never be closed again. Significantly, at the end of the book, she tosses away a gift for Blomkvist in reaction to what she perceives as his betrayal of her, thus ending the book without resolving the romantic plot. (In Chapter Twelve we discuss the benefits of not resolving all the plots at the end of a story.)

Create a Character Emotional Development Plot Profile for Yourself

Take the opportunity to fill in the character profile for yourself as a writer.

Writers' Emotional Development Profile

1. What is your writing goal?
2. What stands in the way of you achieving your writing goal?
3. What do you stand to lose if you are not successful?
4. Name some of your flaws as they have to do with your writing.
5. Name some of your strengths.
6. Name some things you hate about writing.
7. Name some things you love about writing.
8. Name some things you fear.
9. Describe a dream or aspiration.
10. Write down a secret no one else knows about you.

Figure 8. Writers' Emotional Development Profile

How and Why Characters Transform

Character flaws are often created in response to a loss of innocence, a loss that occurs before the story starts. The character stores the emotion created by what happened in the backstory. In reaction, she often surrenders some or all of the authority over her own life to someone or something else.

THE WRITER'S WAY

To better understand the concept of a backstory and perhaps shine a light on the possible influences your own backstory may have on you as a writer and on your writing, write your own history. Search for an event or situation that happened to you, likely several years ago (possibly in your childhood), that represents a loss of innocence. It may have been as dramatic as external violence inflicted on you by a loved one or it may have been as subtle as an overheard conversation.

Look for a memory that has stayed with you, lodged in your psyche in as much detail as the moment it first occurred. This memory does not have to be something huge. Often those big issues have been dealt with over the years. Frequently, it is the smaller events that are more profound. Perhaps on the surface your backstory moment is seemingly benign, but it has affected in a negative way how you view the world.

Write that.

The writer in my workshop absorbed what had happened to her character in his backstory. As a result he now (in the front story) held beliefs or exhibited behavior that reflected a deep psychological issue (flaw). This flaw thwarted his quest for what he desired. Along the way, conflict, tension, suspense, and curiosity in the form of physical, psychological, and spiritual challenges or ordeals created not only page-turning dramatic action, but they challenged the character with possible failure, or even death.

Facing failure (fear) demands courage and faith. Each new and challenging situation forces self-confrontation. The plot begins to reveal inner patterns, developed as a consequence of the character's unexamined backstory. Questioning and discoveries lead characters to overcome shortcomings and develop strengths.

And in the end, as a result of the action on the page, the protagonist of a story *changes*.

PLOT WHISPER

Write the protagonist's backstory in one concise scene.

Keep in mind that as important as the backstory can be in showing who the character is now and as much time as you put into developing it, the protagonist's backstory is not the story. The front story, shown in moment-by-moment dramatic action, is what you're writing about.

A character's emotions and beliefs, originating in her backstory, drive her actions and create the external dramatic action front story. The external plot transforms the internal plot. At the same time, how the character feels inside and what she believes directly impact the outcome of a story.

Keep the backstory scene stored off to the side of your plot planner—don't attach it to the plot planner line itself. After all, the plot planner is intended to plot out the front story, not the backstory. You don't want to get them confused.

How to Convey Emotion in a Character

If your readers are going to read your story all the way to the end, they need to understand and care about the characters. The action has to be exciting, and there has to be meaning attached to the writing. What people most identify with, however, is the character(s). The most complete way for a reader to identify and relate to a character is through the range of emotions exhibited by that character.

The ancient Greeks called on the Muses to grace the world with qualities of living presence: emotion. In a world that is left-brain dominated and heavily influenced by the left-brain specialties of logic, literal interpretation, and other features of the mind, displays of emotion are often frowned upon. We learn to mask our feelings and protect ourselves. This leads us to the mistaken belief that when we experience strong emotions we are the only ones to do so.

Genuine emotions are universal and recognizable even between people who do not share the same language or customs.

Every honest show of emotion by the protagonist renews the Universal Story.

Character Emotional Development Versus Character Emotion

Character emotional development and character emotion each are essential scene elements. The two sound alike. They are related and are often confused.

CHARACTER EMOTIONAL DEVELOPMENT

The protagonist's emotional development takes place over time and culminates at the end of the story in a lasting transformation. The character's emotional development can be plotted from the beginning to the end of the story.

CHARACTER EMOTION

In every scene, the protagonist displays emotion in reaction to the dramatic action. How she reacts often is reflective of the burden she carries from her backstory. These emotions, which fluctuate within each scene, are usually transitory and fleeting.

After the beginning of the story, the protagonist moves out of her familiar surroundings (whether physical or mental) into a new and complex world. The farther the protagonist penetrates into this new world, the more obstacles she confronts. Unable to function at a superficial level any longer, she begins to experience heightened emotions, ones that touch the core of her being. When she is prevented from reaching her goal, her emotional reaction changes subtly over time, flicking back and forth in the scene like a trapped fly.

By the middle of *The Kite Runner* by Khaled Hosseini, the protagonist, Amir, remains stuck in his character emotional development where he has been since the beginning of the book—passive and unable to stand up for himself. This flaw embodies the thematic significance of the story—a man who won't stand up for himself becomes a man who can't stand up to anything, a defect that he must eventually overcome.

The following conversation occurs between Rahim, an old family friend, and Amir after his arrival in Afghanistan, having been summoned by Rahim.

"You know all those years I lived in your father's house after you left?"

"Yes."

"I wasn't alone for all of them. Hassan lived there with me."

"Hassan," I said. When was the last time I had spoken his name? Those thorny old barbs of guilt bore into me once more, as if speaking his name had broken a spell, set them free to torment me anew. Suddenly the air in Rahim Khan's little flat was too thick, too hot, too rich with the smell of the street.

"I thought about writing you and telling you before, but I wasn't sure you wanted to know. Was I wrong?"

The truth was no. The lie was yes. I settle for something in between.

"I don't know."

Amir's response is emblematic of his character emotional development: he always takes the passive route. The suffocation he experiences in

Rahim's little flat is an emotional reaction to being reminded of his past. The feeling is not new. It reflects the burden he carries from his backstory.

Later in the conversation, Amir again reacts emotionally as he understands for the first time his true relationship to Hassan. This moment represents his character emotional development crisis.

> I felt like a man sliding down a steep cliff, clutching at shrubs and tangles of brambles and coming up empty-handed. The room was swooping up and down, swaying side to side. "Did Hassan know?" I said through lips that didn't feel like my own. Rahim Khan closed his eyes. Shook his head.
>
> "You bastards," I muttered. Stood up. "You goddamn bastards!" I screamed.

A pattern emerges in the story, like that you may have experienced when staring at certain paintings. When you look closely at them, they seem confusing constructions of randomly selected colors and slapdash brushstrokes. But as you step away from the canvas, they resolve themselves into complicated compositions that reveal a serene slice of life. In the same way, in a plot every emotion in every scene contributes thematically to the sum of the parts: the overall character transformation that is the goal of the story. Character emotion can turn stagnant, flat scenes into vital and complex ones. The emotion does not have to be monumental but it must communicate true feeling.

PLOT WHISPER

Track the emotional range of your protagonist on the sticky notes hanging above each energetic marker on your plot planner. Examine the overall emotional pattern of your story.

For instance, in the Millenium trilogy by Stieg Larsson, Lisbeth Salander's surface affect is essentially flat but her actions leave no doubt about how she is feeling.

Show, Don't Tell

Emotions, more than almost any other element of writing, require that we go back to the age-old writers' mantra: show, don't tell. You need to show the character's emotions through his or her actions rather than simply telling the reader how he or she feels.

Showing an emotional reaction true to the protagonist is more difficult than merely telling how the protagonist is feeling. How the protagonist holds her body, the tone of her voice, the message she speaks, and the actions she takes offer clues about her emotional response to the action or dialogue around her.

In *The Accidental Tourist* by Anne Tyler, Macon, the protagonist, is a travel writer who hates to travel and despises anything out of the ordinary. His wife recently left him after their young son died. He is behind on his writing deadline.

> In September, he decided to alter his system of dressing. If he wore sweat suits at home—the zipper-free kind, nothing to scratch or bind him—he could go from one shower to the next without changing clothes. The sweat suit would serve as both pajamas and day wear . . . Around noon of the second day, though, he started feeling a little low. He was sitting at his typewriter and something made him notice his posture—stooped and sloppy. He rose and went to the full-length mirror in the hall. His reflection reminded him of a patient in a mental hospital . . . He felt much worse in the morning. It had been a warm night and he woke up sticky and cross. He couldn't face the thought of popcorn for breakfast.

Macon's choices are uniquely representative of his inner character and also show universally recognizable emotions. Yes, we are told he "started feeling a little low" and "felt much worse in the morning" which is telling, yet the author goes on to show him sticky and cross. That he is reduced to eating popcorn for breakfast speaks volumes about how this man is feeling.

Always express the emotion through the character's body or voice. Tone, volume, facial expressions, and body language are universally recognized signals of emotion.

Nonverbal communication expresses emotion. Some examples include:

- Tears
- Laughter
- Gestures
- Eloquent silences
- Breathing
- Pulse
- Moisture on the skin
- Movement of the eyebrows
- Eyes and pupil size
- Muscle tension
- Weight shifts
- Movement of the feet

- Spatial relationships
- Hand gestures
- Body movements though space
- Body posture
- Sensuous and exact details
- Tone of voice
- Mood
- Metaphor

Without some show of emotion, cardboard figures can advance the dramatic action plot, but it won't be compelling.

PLOT WHISPER

Use the following labels to explore emotional expression:

Exhausted, confused, ecstatic, guilty, suspicious, angry, hysterical, frustrated, sad, confident, embarrassed, happy, mischievous, disgusted, frightened, enraged, ashamed, cautious, smug, depressed, overwhelmed, hopeful, lonely, love struck, jealous, bored, surprised, anxious, shocked, shy, acceptance, joy, love, aversion, courage, hate, surprise, pleasure, anxiety, expectancy, contempt, nervous, exasperated, elated, empowered, fearful, achievement, amusement, sensual pleasure.

Write a behavior using one of the nonverbal expressions of emotion listed above. Show without telling how the character feels. Do this to evoke each of the labels.

The pattern of emotional change in the protagonist may be magnified or diminished based on the needs of each individual story, but emotion is always present.

Three-Part Emotion

Scenes ripe for emotional expression by the protagonist occur just before each energetic marker and directly after it. One scene prepares and sets up anticipation in something coming. A follow-up scene shows the full impact of the event on the character—both physically and emotionally. Keep this sequence in mind:

1. Preparation and anticipation
2. Energetic marker and main event
3. Reaction and follow-through

Preparation and anticipation create emotion. A feared event is often worse in your imagination than the actual event itself. Preparation and anticipation generate tension, conflict, and suspense.

The story moves from scene to scene through cause and effect. Conflict in a scene represents the motivating cause that sets a series of events in motion. The character's reaction to those events represents the effect the conflict has on the character. The character responds to the conflict. That response becomes the cause of the next action, which follows with an effect. Each time the character succeeds or fails as she goes after her specific goals, show her emotional reaction to her success or failure. Every part plays into the whole, and you end up with a satisfying story.

Showing the emotional effect the dramatic action has on the character during and after the main event allows the reader to feel the emotions, too. We learn a lot about each other and ourselves by seeing what motivates a character's choices in response to individual events. Build the discomfort scene-by-scene and the reader gains a better and deeper insight into the protagonist's character emotional development.

To depict character emotion beyond the clichés—slamming things and shouting when angry, or dancing and singing when joyful—means thinking about your own experiences with the emotion. Often emotional upheaval manifests itself in far more subtle signs and actions.

THE WRITER'S WAY

Art is involved in conveying how people reveal their emotions. Get it right and your words produce an emotional impact and visceral response in readers and audiences.

Write beyond a simple label and identifiable physical changes. Slip behind the veil to the universality of actually sharing feelings.

Our range of emotions, including love, compassion, confidence, hope, despair, hate, envy, and fear, narrows as we grow into adulthood and are challenged to generate within ourselves an emotional steadiness. What particularly narrows is the range of emotions we permit ourselves to show.

When you reach obstacles in your life, note how you feel and how those inner feelings manifest themselves in your internal and external behavior. Use your findings to help inform your story's emotional weight.

In real life, we are not always encouraged to acknowledge our true emotions. Many of us are taught to be the peacemakers at all cost, to sweep raw, edgy emotions out of sight of others, and often to keep silent ourselves so as not to provoke and exacerbate touchy situations. No wonder so many people have difficulty displaying and even acknowledging human emotions in themselves, let alone showing emotions in their characters in true and fresh ways. Gen Xers and more recent generations, who have been encouraged to explore feelings and express them more honestly, show indications that it may be easier for younger writers to conjure up unique shows of emotion in their characters.

Remember:

- At the beginning of a story, the character's emotional reactions help identify and introduce the character.
- In the middle of a story, the character's emotional defenses begin to break down and her emotions turn bleaker and darker.
- At the end of a story, the character's transformation is revealed through the change in her choices and in her emotional responses from how she acted in the beginning and in the middle.

A character's emotional reactions as a response to dramatic action incidents deepen the readers' understanding of the inner life of the character. When we know how the conflict emotionally affects the character, we care about the story.

PLOT WHISPER

Keep your journal with you at all times to jot down behaviors you see in others or feel in yourself that signify emotional reaction to external events. Push yourself to detect emotional displays, no matter how subtle, beyond clichés.

The more outside the norm you write your protagonist's emotional makeup, the more unique your story and the more deeply readers will connect emotionally to the character and the dramatic action of your story.

CHAPTER SIX
WHO OPPOSES THE PROTAGONIST?

One may smile, and smile, and be a villain.

—Shakespeare, *Hamlet*, Act 1, Scene V

As we've seen with the aid of our plot planners, the energy of the Universal Story rises and falls. Antagonists, because their role in stories is to prevent or delay the protagonist from successfully reaching her goal, always cause the energy to rise.

Imagine a story as a conflict between energies of light and dark. They shift back and forth between the protagonist and the antagonists. The antagonists represent darkness as they strive to keep the protagonist as she currently exists. The protagonist represents the light in the struggle to evolve. Change is never easy, and a protagonist bound in the darkness of her backstory and locked in repetitive patterns dictated by her flaw will necessarily struggle. When the protagonist pushes toward her desire, she directs the energy. Internal and external forces (antagonists) push against her.

A protagonist who wants something enough to take action against all the antagonists within and without creates a story.

External Antagonists

Any external person, place, or thing that stands in the way of the protagonist seizing what she desires constitutes an external antagonist.

101

PLOT WHISPER

Make a list of the major antagonists preventing your protagonist from reaching her goal. Include people, places, objects, machinery, natural features, and concepts or beliefs in the list.

Add to the energetic markers on your plot planner the external antagonists in control at each of the major turning points of your story. Give any antagonist that consistently reappears throughout the story and poses a significant challenge to the protagonist its own sticky note color.

Begin now to add other scenes to your plot planner in the same manner as you did for the energetic markers. Plot dramatic action scenes where an antagonist is in control above the line on a plot planner, using the appropriate dramatic action plot sticky note color. Include the effect the antagonist's external actions have on the protagonist on the correct colored sticky notes for the character emotional development plot.

Scenes where an antagonist holds the power over the protagonist create more energy than do scenes where the protagonist is safe and calm. Scenes where the antagonist holds the power belong above the line. Plot the scenes in which the protagonist is in charge below the line. Scenes above the plot planner line keep the story moving. Scenes below the line slow the story.

Stand back. Determine the flow of energy between the protagonist and the antagonists; see where and how the energy surges. Assess the flow of energy in all the scenes put together for your story's overall intensity level.

Antagonists, as I remarked above, can be animate or inanimate. Either way they pose a series of tough challenges to the protagonist's long-term goal of transformation. We can see this working in *Outlander*, the first in a series of epic romance novels by Diana Gabaldon. At the outset, we find ourselves in 1945. Claire Randall, the protagonist of the story and former combat nurse in World War II, has returned from the war and is reunited with her husband on a second honeymoon. Suddenly she finds herself mysteriously transported to 1743 Scotland, a country torn by war and raiding border clans.

The set-up of the story gives the reader plenty of clues to the antagonists in the story. A primary antagonist is the time travel itself, which snatches Claire from 1945 and catapults her into Scotland just prior to the Highland uprising to restore the Stewart kings to the throne of England. Claire's stated goal upon entering the exotic world of lairds and spies is to find a way to return to her husband and her own time.

Claire meets a gallant young Scottish warrior, James Fraser, who becomes the major male character and represents the essence of the novel's romance plot. In the first part of the middle of the story, James represents a major antagonist. Though later in the story he changes when he shows love for Claire, he presents the ultimate challenge to her long-term goal of returning to her husband and the 1940s.

PLOT WHISPER

For any character in your story who acts as a villain, cut out a magazine picture that represents the antagonist. Or, use a photo of someone you know who embodies the strengths and flaws you envision for the character. You can choose an actor whom you could envision playing the role of the antagonist. Affix these visual representations of your main antagonists on your plot planner to stimulate ideas.

Internal Antagonists

Of all the antagonists available to you, those that represent the inner workings of the protagonist herself offer the richest area for development.

Three of these in particular have the potential to create scenes that resonate with conflict, tension, suspense, or curiosity: the protagonist's flaw, fear, and hatred.

The protagonist's flaw interferes with her attaining her goal—the very definition of an antagonist. In other words, *the protagonist acts as her own antagonist* each time she prevents herself from moving forward. This type of antagonist is especially powerful and connects emotionally with readers because many of us recognize how much we stand in the way of our own happiness.

The protagonist must overcome her flaw and release the consequent flood of emotion in order for her character to transform and the story to end.

We all have fears that derive from universal emotions. The protagonist's fears can be sparked by an external foe—anything from an irritable parent to a malfunctioning robot. Anytime that foe is mentioned or present, the energy of the scene surges and creates a sense of anticipation: *will she survive or will she be crushed?* The more powerful the character, the more powerful the external force.

Other fears are divorced from any concrete and immediate danger and are about something that *could* happen. They create tension in the protagonist as she wonders when and how those internal fears will affect the action of the external story. Fear of failure, fear of being hurt, fear of making the wrong decision, fear of loss, fear of death—all these keep the protagonist disconnected from her true power. What she fears gives the reader insight into her emotional makeup and points to what she must ultimately confront in order to transform.

Hate is a powerful negative emotion. When caught up in it, the protagonist is never in control of the emotion; rather, it controls her. This is true whether what she hates is external—another person, a job, a situation—or internal—her choices, her thoughts, her beliefs. Every scene in which the character is directly confronted by that which she most hates creates conflict, tension, and suspense. Every scene in which the threat of what the protagonist hates hovers nearby creates anxiety in the reader. Sooner or later this emotion will have to be faced and ultimately relinquished.

The Antagonist's Goal

Whether a spiritual belief or a coping strategy, a physical ailment or society at large, every antagonist has one primary goal within the context of the story: to prevent or delay the protagonist from successfully reaching her goal.

Your goal as the writer is to keep the energy of the story surging, boiling, and spitting enticements to the protagonist to return to the easy way, the comfort of the past as she pushes forward to a new and truly different future.

An antagonist in the story doesn't have to consciously intend to hold back the protagonist's transformation. If asked, he might reply that his goal is simply to take his wife out to dinner, give an employee a raise, or cleanse a believer of her sins. The question is not about his intentions but about their effect. Whatever actions the antagonist takes or whatever feelings he inspires, the outcome initially will be to prevent the protagonist from reaching her goal.

A villain, a more or less conscious antagonist, intends not only to prevent the protagonist from reaching her goal; his goal is to steal her goal for himself.

A villain is always an antagonist, but not all antagonists are villains.

PLOT WHISPER
Fill out a Character Emotional Development Plot Profile for all major antagonists in your story.

How the Protagonist and Antagonists Interact

Antagonists wreak havoc throughout a story and especially so in the middle. Antagonists appear in full force when the protagonist moves into a new and different world. They disorient and shake up the protagonist; she swings wildly from one emotional extreme to another. If that happens in your story, take comfort. Antagonists are designed to knock your protagonist down, mess her up, and turn her life around.

The deeper the protagonist ventures into this new world, the more intense the energy of the dramatic action as the antagonists work more rigorously to block her forward movement.

THE WRITER'S WAY

Antagonists begin appearing in your new writing world. They may be old friends or new, harboring their own private reasons to divert you, disorient you, and shake you up. Under the circumstances, you may feel driven to bully and control someone or something.

Beware. Do not turn on your story.

Steer clear of your own ego in this brave new world you have entered. See yourself as the sole creator of this story and your ego will produce an imbalance. See yourself as the conduit and your cooperation leads to balance.

Guide the story along the parameters you have planned. In the first few drafts, do not let your analytical mind offer suggestions, changes, or improvements. Over the past weeks, your analytical mind has served you well as you plotted, planned, schemed, and researched. But the moment you crossed the threshold and began to actually write, your analytic mind shifted from ally to antagonist.

Do not slow down. Stay in the moment of the writing itself. Your story lives within you.

Learn to see the antagonists as reflections of who you are now in your journey. Rather than despairing and feeling victimized, explore the meaning of the antagonists in your life. Such an exploration leads to transformation.

CREATE CURIOSITY

Action caused by an antagonist always creates conflict, tension, and suspense in the minds of your readers. Although they think they know how the protagonist will react, they are curious what aspects the protagonist will reveal of herself. Antagonists operate as mirrors to the protagonist by revealing those parts of her that need to be healed.

For each of the antagonists in the list you created, indicate the elements of the protagonist they represent, such as fear, strength, flaw, love, hatred, prejudice, and the like.

Antagonists Generate Emotion

People who read and go to the movies enjoy watching a character's emotional reaction to the challenges that face her. The reader experiences the protagonist's emotions on a visceral level as the protagonist finds her way. Employ as many antagonists as necessary to display a depth and breadth of emotions in your protagonist. Your story takes on greater meaning the deeper she travels into the Universal Story.

The tougher and cleverer the challenges and confrontations created by the antagonists, the greater will be the protagonist's eventual transformation. When she stares down her greatest fear and seizes her prize, she wins. And the reader wins.

Nature as an Antagonist

As I previously indicated, not all antagonists are people. Nature itself can be a formidable antagonist—monumental as a flood, a hurricane, or an earthquake. Nature as an antagonist can work on a more subtle level, too. Nature equals Mother Earth, which in turn represents the creative force and the Universal Story. Because the protagonist is powerless to control nature, she either resists or surrenders to it. Nature as an antagonist creates mood and adds depth to the thematic significance of the conflict, tension, and suspense. The Dust Bowl that forces the Joad family to start their road trip to California signifies the drying up of the family's way of life. The tornado that sweeps up Dorothy and lands her in Oz is symbolic of the swirling emotions the young girl feels about her life in Kansas.

Rather than treat natural events as random occurrences in the plot, assign them deliberate meaning in each scene and in the overall story. Nature awakens primal emotions in both characters and readers. Take advantage of this.

Nature unfolds through the four seasons. It is essential in every scene to ground the reader by revealing where the scene takes place and when. This includes the season of the year, the day of the week, and time of day. Factors within nature that challenge the protagonist add conflict and tension; they push scenes above the plot planner line.

Dawn and dusk are often considered the "between times" when the veil between the physical and the unmanifested, the past and the future grows thin. These times create poignancy, melancholy, and sometimes a sense of imbalance. Throw in the haunting cry of a mourning dove or the howl of a lone wolf and the feeling intensifies.

Often the antagonist of nature collides with the antagonist of society. For example, a character faces the holidays at the end of the year alone. Depending on the protagonist's emotional development, such a time can evoke emotion in the reader or moviegoer in a way no other time of the year is able to do. This emotion intensifies when the weather turns violent, reflecting the character's inner turmoil.

The search for just the right antagonists is as important to the character's emotional development as the search for authentic details is to the thematic significance of a story.

Use of Adversity in Stories

Adversity does not build character. It reveals what was already there.

Antagonists create adversity in order to reveal who the character truly is. The deeper the protagonist travels into the middle of the story, the more nuances are revealed in her emotional development. If you have held back before, bring on the antagonists in the middle and thrust the protagonist into conflict. This will help you emphasize her flawed nature at this stage in her progress through the Universal Story.

The Role of Supporting Characters

Just as subplots complement the primary plot, every secondary character functions as a mirror reflecting back to the protagonist the very elements she spots in others but is blind to in herself. Every secondary character, however minor, whether an antagonist, ally, friend, lover, or a combination of them has something to teach, awaken, challenge, and love in the protagonist.

THE WRITER'S WAY

The greatest gift you can give a story is the courage to allow the protagonist and yourself to fail, appear foolish, lonely, tedious, or ordinary. Until a character experiences failure, brokenness, fear, emptiness, and alienation, the alchemy of change cannot occur.

Rather than retreat, this is the time to crank up the energy. Do not fall prey to the mistaken belief that by making a commitment, the hard work is behind you or you will step forward into thin air and fall with a resounding thud.

The pressure of putting a character into more and more peril and exposing her to more and more unhappiness is many a talented writer's undoing. Write through your doubt and fear as the protagonist struggles and resists. In so doing, all the while, she unknowingly and repeatedly surrenders her will to the antagonists.

As your protagonist recommits to her goal, you, too, recommit to yours.

First, decide who will tell the story. Remain consistent about which point of view will dominate the story. If you tell the story from one character's point of view, do not insert the thoughts or feelings of another character into the narrative beyond what the narrator interprets them to be.

Readers connect to one character at a time. Often they resist leaving the point-of-view character. A clear first line for each switch in point of view creates a minimum of confusion. Then when readers are pulled into the next character's mind and body, they have little reason to feel they will miss the character they just were connected to.

THE WRITER'S WAY

Perhaps you are fortunate enough to have a lifestyle that supports writing and reading, and you can fully sink into the writer's life. Perhaps for years you have written, but because you think as if fireworks were going off in your brain, ideas flying in all different directions at once, every writing session feels as if you are embarking on yet another new story.

Now, by sticking up the notes on a plot planner, you find it easier to focus on one story line. You see where you are headed and why. You find yourself sticking to a plan. Slowly the uncertainty you feel in the blind pursuit of your dream is being replaced with confidence.

Be cautious as you reach the halfway point of your story. You're about to reach a transition point. At the halfway point you must fully commit to the story.

Even if you are shaky about some of the elements and completely uncertain about the outcome, do not let another half-written story end up in the trash bin or at the bottom of a cabinet drawer. But, how do I make it all the way to the end, you ask?

With grace and splendor? A true writer's journey is messier. Commit to your own hero's journey as your protagonist embarks on hers.

Through the process of learning about your character, learn about what and to whom you give over authority for yourself. Who and what represent your greatest antagonists?

Recognize the similarities. Push yourself. See what happens.

In the first quarter of *When the Killing's Done* by T. C. Boyle, two characters alternate chapters told from their own points of view. The beginning chapters of the story are Alma's introduction told through her grandmother's story. The third chapter focuses on Alma herself and begins by firmly grounding the reader.

> Though Alma is trying her hardest to suppress it, the noise of the freeway is getting to her. She can't think to slice the cherry tomatoes and dice the baby carrots, can't clear her head, can barely hear Micah Stroud riding the tide of his emotions through the big speakers in the front room.

These two sentences immediately thrust the reader into the scene. They show who is doing what, how the action is emotionally affecting her, and a general idea where she is. They also offer specific details that define Alma: living near a noisy freeway, knowing how to cook, listening to music that rides the tide of the singer's emotions, and loving music enough that she owns big speakers.

The next chapter switches to the male character's point of view.

> If there is one thing he hates, it's a runny yolk.

That's about all the reader needs in order to know the main character in this chapter. He's opinionated and narrow minded.

NEVER REPEAT, DEEPEN

Throughout a story, the protagonist interacts more than once with other characters. The reappearance of the antagonist gives you an opening. Do not repeat the previous interaction; instead, make it more complex and give a deeper understanding of the protagonist's emotional development.

This is true for all your characters. Each time one of them reappears, it gives the reader a deeper glimpse into the character—strengths, weaknesses, and all.

A writer in one of my workshops introduced the protagonist's long-term goal of wanting to advance in her career and make more money. The character's flaw was that she was a gossip. The writer created scenes in the beginning of the project that showed the character trying to impress her boss. At the same time, these scenes presented her character flaw and some of its consequences. Showing the character as a gossip when the stakes involved in such actions are relatively small allows for a greater story arc that will show the overall growth of the character.

The protagonist had several meetings in the boardroom with the boss. Each scene provided opportunities to increase the energy in the dramatic action and also to expand the character's emotional development. To achieve this expansion, the writer began to show how the flaw affected the character's work life. Subsequent scenes showed how her flaw affected her relationships, her health, and her mental well-being. Each scene expanded the consequences of this flaw, as well as the character's gradual recognition of the contradictions and challenges in her world.

In the middle of the story, the protagonist met with a coworker, a secondary character whom she had encountered in the beginning of the story. Rather than deepen the readers' appreciation for the character's emotional development, however, at this point the writer essentially repeated the scene from the beginning of the story.

As a way to increase tension and conflict in the scene with the coworker, I suggested the writer brainstorm ideas that showed the growing effects the flaw had on the protagonist's behavior as she advanced in her job. The protagonist strove toward her goal, confronted by an antagonist (the coworker), and exhibited her flawed behavior. This time, however, the protagonist's actions had greater, more wide-ranging consequences.

In this way, each time the protagonist's flaw manifested itself, the reader's perception of what this flaw looks like in all its forms expanded. Each scene in which the character displayed her flaw showed her in a new light, both to the reader and, eventually, to herself.

Throughout the beginning and middle portions of the story, the character was naïve and oblivious, unaware that she fit the description of a gossip. At the crisis, however, she finally got it. After that came her steady climb toward transformation.

PLOT OUT SECONDARY CHARACTER ROLES

Some subplots and secondary characters deserve their own plot planners. In that case, draw one line above the other to assess the interdependence between the characters and how they work with the primary dramatic action plot and the character emotional development plot.

Think, for a moment, of how to meet the challenge of effective secondary characters. Imagine that you've written the rough draft of a murder mystery, primarily focusing on the dramatic action plot. You've toyed around with the underlying meaning of the story, its thematic significance.

You receive feedback from an editor or your critique group. Two secondary characters do not provide any depth or meaning; they need development.

Early in your draft, you considered a romance between the protagonist and the detective. In middle-grade fiction, this might translate to a friendship challenge. In a murder mystery, it can become a partnership challenge. A romantic plot line reveals a personal aspect of the protagonist that extends beyond the dramatic action plot.

In the next draft, concentrate on plotting out a romantic challenge. This doesn't mean switching your genre to romance (though romance is the hottest-selling genre in the world). For a romance novel, the primary plot revolves around two individuals falling in love and struggling to make the relationship work. That is not what your mystery story is about.

Explore and expand the interactions between one of the secondary characters, an investigative detective, and the protagonist. As written now, the protagonist and detective meet several times over coffee to discuss the case. The relationship goes nowhere, there's no tension, no conflict, and no curiosity.

In the revised version, the protagonist and detective grow closer, although their time together is fraught with misunderstanding, frustrations, conflict, tension, and suspense. In the end, the character's confidence about developing the relationship serves as a metaphor for the confidence you, the writer, feel in yourself.

Fill out a character emotional profile for the two questionable secondary characters. Keep up your original plot planner and use it to plot out each of the secondary characters' plotlines. Place one above the other and both above the original plotline for the protagonist's emotional development and dramatic action plot.

1. Stick color-coded notes (one color for each character) at every scene where the secondary characters are present as the story stands now.
2. Analyze these appearances—their frequency and location.
3. Plot out a story line for each character in much the same way you did the primary challenge or the protagonist's character emotional development plotline.
   - A secondary character goes after a goal (note: the more closely related thematically to the primary plot and at odds with her inner plot, the better).
   - The secondary character is thwarted at every turn and interferes with the protagonist's progress.

Secondary characters enhance the primary story and contribute to the meaning of the piece overall.

THE WRITER'S WAY

If you suddenly find your story is littered with plotlines and sub-plots, flashbacks and time jumps, you may be suffering from a common problem among writers: you are trying too hard.

Ask yourself: Who is going to read this? And why? In your fear that the story falls short, you add another subplot here, switch events around, change the point-of-view, and mess with the linear format.

These questions and fears constitute part of the writer's personal journey. Your ego keeps your mind so filled with fear and uncertainty that you trip over the story itself. The writer's craft is to take what flows out on the page and form it into a story. So long as you focus on the story, you'll get it right. Get in the way, and the process bogs down. When you try too hard, you tense up. The story tenses up, too.

Return to your plot planner and reconnect with the core or heart of your story itself. Examine the themes and the deeper meaning of the story. In viewing your stories minus the words, you can see a story worth the time and attention it is going to take to get it right.

Stubbornness (perseverance), ambition (practice), and individuality (exploration) get you far as a writer. Every time you recommit to your story, you figuratively and symbolically discover new and creative solutions for achieving your goals.

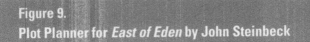

Figure 9.
Plot Planner for *East of Eden* by John Steinbeck

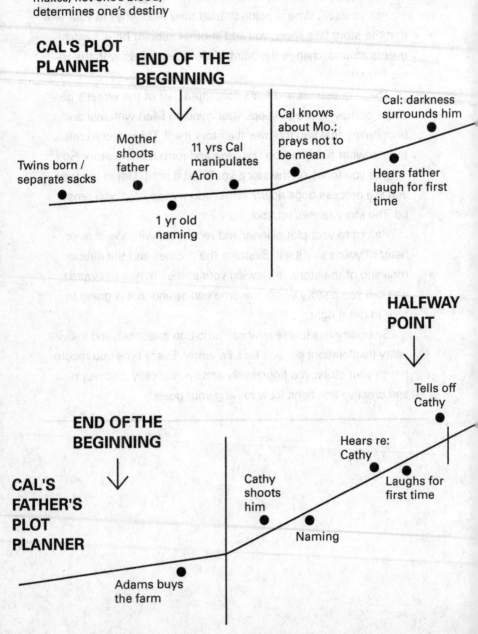

Theme: The choices one makes, not one's blood, determines one's destiny

CAL'S PLOT PLANNER

END OF THE BEGINNING

Twins born / separate sacks

1 yr old naming

Mother shoots father

11 yrs Cal manipulates Aron

Cal knows about Mo.; prays not to be mean

Hears father laugh for first time

Cal: darkness surrounds him

HALFWAY POINT

CAL'S FATHER'S PLOT PLANNER

END OF THE BEGINNING

Adams buys the farm

Cathy shoots him

Naming

Hears re: Cathy

Laughs for first time

Tells off Cathy

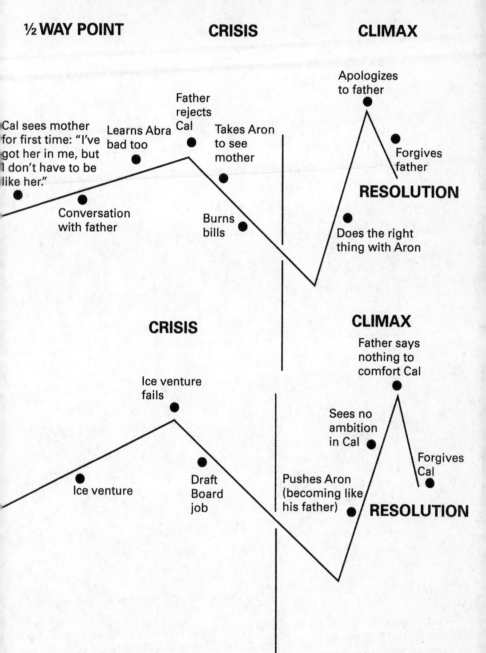

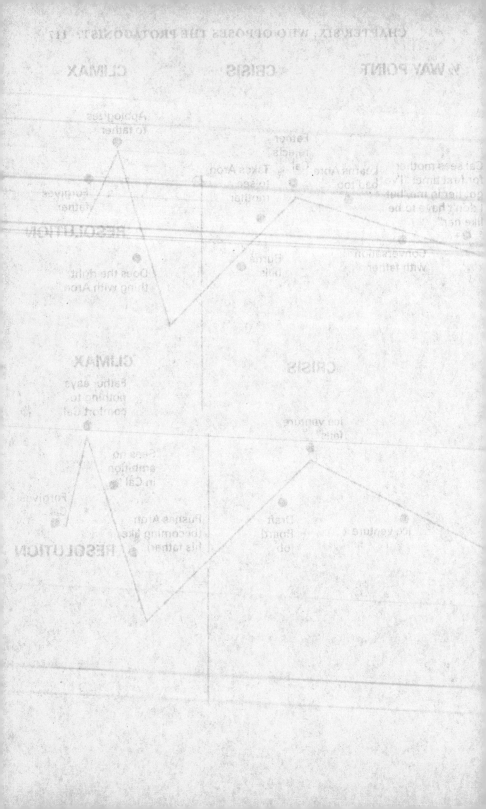

CHAPTER SEVEN

THE DEVIL'S IN THE DETAILS

If there's a book you really want to read but it hasn't been written yet, then you must write it.

—Toni Morrison

Abstractions and generalizations lock a story at a surface level and keep readers at arm's length. Concrete and sensory details, on the other hand, penetrate to where emotion lies. They invite readers and audiences to think, to feel, and to actively participate in the story you tell.

Readers who believe you in the details up front will believe you in the bigger things to come.

What Setting Is Appropriate?

Stories generally have at least two major settings.

The reader meets the protagonist in her usual environment, which defines the beginning quarter of the story. Stories that begin in the protagonist's ordinary world satisfy two important elements of beginnings: introduction and grounding.

Upon entering the middle of the story world, the protagonist is confronted with the second setting: a new and exotic world. The more unusual the new world is in its surroundings, mind-set, and demands upon the protagonist, the more unusual are her experiences, explorations, endurance, and quest for survival.

ORDINARY WORLD SETTING

A story is about a character transformed over time by the dramatic action. In order to make this character transformation more dramatic, writers convey who the character is within the safety of a world that is familiar to her before she is thrust into a new world.

PLOT WHISPER

Cut out of a magazine a picture that represents the setting of the protagonist's ordinary world (her house, community, country, planet, depending on the needs of your particular story). If you can't find something suitable, use a photo of a place you know that embodies the qualities you envision for your protagonist's home, neighborhood, community, and so on. Affix this visual representation of your main character's usual world above the beginning section of your plot planner to stimulate ideas.

The ordinary world gives the reader insight into the values, background, and habits of the protagonist (or lack thereof). Usually the protagonist has a life before the story begins, although some stories such as Ursula Hegi's *Stones from the River* begin on or nearly at the protagonist's birth. The reader, in the first part of the story, gains a sense of the main character's framework of relationships and the degree to which she's governed by them. This gives the reader a starting point from which to evaluate the emotional change in the protagonist as she is forced to break away and rely on herself in the middle of the story.

In her usual life, customs, dogma, rules, and regulations come from outside the protagonist. They often form a kind of inner protection for her. In the middle of the story when this protection is stripped away, she becomes vulnerable. If we grasp the comfortable, safe, and well-fed environment the protagonist has always known, it's easier for us to sympathize when she wonders why she left it in pursuit of a solitary, difficult, and dangerous new world.

EXOTIC WORLD SETTING

For a character to transform, she must take a journey. It can be physical: on a train through the Alps or across the Sahara on a camel. Or it can be internal: a movement away from comfort and into the great unknown. (It can, of course, be both.) Throughout the middle of the story, the protagonist is exposed to the otherness of the new and exotic world in the form of differing cultures, personalities, ideas, value systems, landscapes, and languages.

The exotic world itself creates tension, conflict, and suspense merely by its unfamiliarity to the protagonist; thus, it produces a sense of overarching tension. As well, in the new world, the old rules with which the protagonist is familiar and the beliefs she grew up with no longer apply.

PLOT WHISPER

Cut out of a magazine a picture that represents the exotic world your protagonist steps into. If you can't find an appropriate picture, use a photo of somewhere familiar to you that embodies the qualities you envision for the setting that best serves to shake up your protagonist. Affix this visual representation of the exotic world above the middle section of your plot planner to help stimulate ideas.

In the novel *The English Patient* by Michael Ondaatje and screenplay of the same name by film director and screenwriter Anthony Minghella, the authors introduce the time (toward the end of World War II) and setting (an abandoned Italian monastery) in the beginning of the story. The setting is fraught with danger. The fears, flaws, and mysteries about the protagonist create more. The last sentence of the beginning part of the story introduces Kip, an Indian Sikh sapper in the British Army, promising change. This signifies the end of the beginning and the first energetic marker.

The middle begins with Kip, a bomb disposal specialist with a goal to rid the villa of its dangers, going about his business of detecting and defusing live bombs. His actions make real the threats of an uncut fuse wire, pencil mines, glass bombs, and bombs drilled into fruit trees. This builds on what is an unusual setting in the beginning to the exotic world of the middle. Now, upon Kip's arrival, what was an overarching threat of booby traps, land mines, and hidden bombs hangs even heavier. This allows the story to slow down without losing readers' interest as scenes deepen the sense of place, time, and humanness.

The Middle of the Middle

The middle is the longest portion of the project—it constitutes one half of the entire story. It commands the most scenes and is where many writers fall short. The energy in the middle builds, rather than falling, and the significance of each scene rises to the crisis. Conflict, tension, and suspense in the dramatic action and character emotional development intensify scene by scene to the crisis. However, as long as conflict, tension, and curiosity remain alive and create an overarching suspenseful quality to the scenes, the actual dramatic action can often flatten out a bit in the earlier portion of the middle. This gives the reader a moment to catch her breath and relax before plunging into the scenes in the middle of the middle.

In order to help you over the roughest territory—the middle of the middle—develop the new world the protagonist enters into an unusual and richly detailed setting.

By the time most readers reach the middle of a novel or a movie, they are committed to going all the way to the end. Whatever dangers may loom for the protagonist won't happen right away. The reader can sink into the story, enjoy a romp through the exotic world of the middle, hang out, and get to know the characters better.

Choose a setting for the middle that will challenge the protagonist. Locate a setting that stirs wonder, bewilderment, and even disorientation. This should be one that forces the protagonist to reinterpret her belief system, one that is greater and more complex than she ever imagined.

Once you have the right setting, deepen the readers' appreciation of the nuances of the unusual location, job, lifestyle, custom, ritual, sport, beliefs, state of mind, or whatever your imagination dreams up.

The setting, whether real or imagined, that defines the middle of the story comes alive with details most relevant to the unusual world. For example, in the middle of *Memoirs of a Geisha* by Arthur Golden (the screenplay for the film was written by Robin Swicord), the protagonist and the reader learn about such things as "geisha" dance steps, joke making, dress, hair, and makeup.

Nitta Sayuri, the main character whose "memoir" this is, tells the reader, "Following drums, my next lesson of the morning was in Japanese flute, and after that in shamisen. The method in studying any of the instruments was more or less the same. The teacher began by playing something and then the students tried to play it back. On occasion it sounded like a band of animals at the zoo, but not often, because the teachers were careful to begin simply. For example, 'So-and-so, you must keep your little finger down, not up in the air. And you, Such-and-such, does your flute smell bad? Well then, why do you wrinkle your nose that way?' "

The degree of detail in this passage helps us understand the character of geishas as the story unfolds. We learn that they must be skilled in a variety of Japanese musical forms and that their training is very strict.

In the middle of *Where the Wild Things Are*, Maurice Sendak devotes six full pages of illustrations to the unusual world of wild things making rumpus. In the middle of *Sounds Like Crazy*, Shana Mahaffey takes the reader deep into the world of a voice-over star of a new animated television show and impresses upon the reader what life is like coping with five different identities.

THE WRITER'S WAY

The further you venture into the world of writing, the more you find yourself hanging out at bookshops and going to book readings. You love the play of words in dialogue, the freedom, the feeling of being connected to something larger than yourself . . . at first.

The deeper you wade into your story, the more emotional you feel. You examine and question and react to things you always have held dear. Beliefs you once identified with and that gave you a sense of yourself are stripped away. You feel anger and frustration, disappointment and self-pity. You believe yourself to be alone in your shame and self-loathing. You long to run back to the safety of your life before things got so complicated.

What you do not appreciate is that the phase you are in—the middle—is vital to your transformation. You doubt your ability to be creative, imaginative, willing, talented, disciplined, funny, and intelligent. You despair and ask yourself who you are without your old things, beliefs, and ideals. Yet, in truth, everything you need to be successful is being revealed to you already.

A writer and illustrator of picture books on the west coast of California creates a whimsical story about outrageous buttons and bows, a boy, and a princess. The details she uses create immediate mental images of sparkly buttons, frilly bows, and graceful high-heeled shoes.

Her story is good. But rather than step out into an exotic new world and accept an invitation to meet an agent who admires her tale, the writer slips away without a goodbye.

Conveying Sensory Impressions of the Setting

Sense organs relay messages to your brain: the smell of dust on the road, the taste of rust, the heat of the summer sun beating on your skin.

A setting bathed in sights and sounds, language and climate, draws the reader in at the sensory level. Sensory details, fully realized, reinforce the deeper meaning of a story and evoke emotion, which as we've discussed connects a reader to the story.

To help deepen the world of the middle, first identify the details in each scene. Concentrate in particular on the four energetic markers and any other major turning points in your story. The scenes at these markers deserve special treatment. One way to create a scene with greater impact is to engage all five senses.

Details that are fitting for your individual story and, at the same time, are universal draw the reader in and allow her to experience the story as viscerally as does the character. Physical details with historical weight add another layer of significance to a story.

Using Details to Reinforce the Theme and Plot

Physical and sensory details help suspend reality and allow readers to fully involve themselves in the story's environment. The reader's ability to evaluate the significance of the details in the context of the bigger picture of your vision allows you to expand your thematic meaning.

Until you have written a draft or two or three and know the thematic significance of the story overall, use the information you generated in the thematic significance exercise you started in Chapter Four.

The smaller bubbles around the central oval reflect themes as they pop up in the writing of your story. Those themes and, ultimately, the overall thematic significance of your entire story determine how you will write each scene: word choices in dialogue, tone of voice, facial expression, body language, spoken language, music, food, textiles, aromas, and physical objects.

Determine in which scenes an earlier phrase, observation, or use of an object is repeated for thematic weight. Repetitions create pattern recognitions and provide significance. Repeat the same detail again and you establish rhythm.

A detail read 100 pages earlier in the story and repeated reminds the reader and audience of a past experience. The feeling of a shared history with the story's protagonist creates a bond that resonates with readers and audiences long after the story has ended.

Note significant details that occur in your scenes. A detail that appears in the first draft, such as a sound, a color, a movement, or a location, becomes an opportunity to go back later and perfect the detail, giving it a deeper meaning that emerges over time.

F. Scott Fitzgerald uses just the right details in *The Great Gatsby*.

The moon had risen higher, and floating in the Sound was a triangle of silver scales, trembling a little to the stiff, tinny drip of the banjoes on the lawn.

The silver moonlight in this sentence is one of the many examples of Fitzgerald's use of color. Silver and gold (or yellow), colors of wealth, recur again and again in his books, associated especially with vulgar displays of affluence. Daisy's color is white. She wears white dresses and recalls her "white girlhood." This helps characterize her as the unattainable "enchanted princess" who incarnates from Gatsby's dream.

The reader watches the rising moon and hears the tinny drip of the banjoes on the lawn. The details are true to the thematic ground in which the story plays out. At the same time, the words that express those details ring with wealth and affluence. The one tiny reference to "trembling" plants a question about the described rich life with little solace but the beauty of the setting.

DEVELOP DETAILS LIKE DRAFTS

The most original details convey your character's emotional reactions to the dramatic action in the story. In the first draft, as you write all the way through to the end, the details you use are likely generic and clichéd. In each new draft, especially as you come to learn more about the thematic significance of your story, the details become more specific and unique to the story and, at the same time, achingly universal.

PLOT WHISPER

Writers have a tendency to get stuck in their heads, focus on themselves, and look inward rather than outward. They obsess about the stories they write to the point that they often miss the details of the world around them.

Can you remember what you wore yesterday?

What did your significant other wear? What about your children or your best friend?

Close your eyes. How many objects in the room you are sitting in can you describe in detail?

Pull yourself out of a conversation you are having with another person and watch the interchange, as if watching a movie. Memorize the words the other person speaks. Note what she holds back and how she conveys meaning through nonverbal communication.

Recount the last conversation you had. What did the other person say? Your answers, or lack thereof, may surprise you.

Look at the details that surround you. What do they convey about where you are on your writer's journey?

What can you let go of, both tangible and intangible, to move nearer to who you dream of being?

Whenever you are not writing, pay attention to the world around you and what others are saying. Jot down notes in your journal that you carry with you everywhere. Tune into the details of the natural world. The practice gets you out of your head and produces gems for the theme, mood, and nuance of your story.

Most of a writer's genius comes in the art of the finesse. How finely you craft your project before you let it go is up to each individual writer.

The first few drafts are spent developing the overall plot and structure. Until the form of the story works—a likable character, action linked by cause and effect that rises and falls and rises again and all adds up to mean something—finding just the right word in just the right sentence can be premature. Writing a book can drag on forever, because we bury our heads in the words rather than take time to step away and analyze the overall story, the big picture.

RESEARCH FOR AUTHENTIC DETAILS

To find just the right word and just the right details demands you know the setting of your story intimately. This applies to both the ordinary world at the beginning and the exotic world in the middle.

Novelists who rely only on their imaginations to dream up the finer details end up sounding superficial and vague. Memoirists often mistakenly dig only in their memories for details of the day. Rather than creating a sense of authority about their story worlds, these writers end up with general and stereotypical details. Research hones the choices down to the exact right, concrete, definitive, and specific detail.

Beware! Researching also acts as a stimulus. After one research session, a tiny detail can inspire hours of writing. Research can also seduce you deeper and deeper into details, amassing more and more choices, and taking you further and further away from your writing goal. Historical facts and ideas stimulate creativity. They can also bury you alive. *As long as you are writing, do not stop to research. First, finish the draft all the way to the end.*

In its first drafts, a story settles into an overall plot made up of the four energetic markers and turning points, character growth and transformation, and an overall theme. In each rewrite you turn more attention to getting every word perfect.

Wait until you have written your story all the way through to the end a few times before concentrating on the use of language, metaphors, and details. Using every word perfectly takes attention to detail and demands a different mind-set than does generating the initial story.

Details shape the reader's attention and judgment. Describing a character's clothes as shabby, torn, and faded conveys a vastly different reality than if you describe those clothes as crisp, ironed, and bright. Saying they look scrubbed and mended gives yet a different impression of the character. Ballet slippers may perfectly identify your protagonist. However, adding that the shoes are pink satin toe-shoes deepens the experience by evoking the added physical sensations of touch and feel.

In *Memoirs of a Geisha*, the protagonist unwraps a gift given her by the best friend of the Chairman, the man she secretly loves.

> I felt very embarrassed with everyone watching, but I unfolded the paper wrapping and opened the little wooden box inside to find an exquisite ornamental comb on a bed of satin. The comb, in the shape of a half-circle, was a showy red color adorned with bright flowers.
>
> "It's an antique I found a few days ago," Nobu said.
>
> The Chairman, who was gazing wistfully at the ornament in its box on the table, moved his lips, but no sound came out first, until he cleared his throat and then said, with a strange sort of sadness, "Why, Nobu-san. I had no idea you were so sentimental."

This passage expands the reader's understanding of the customs and culture of the exotic world of geishas. The gift is elegant and expensive—wooden box with a bed of satin. That the comb is ornamental and not practical reinforces the extravagance of the gift. As readers absorb the tiny details that contribute to the larger picture of the entire story, they are also given insight into a shift in the romance plot as the Chairman's best friend and the man who saved his life gives the gift as a declaration of his intentions for the woman the Chairman loves.

Track your scenes from the very first paragraph of your story for meaningful and memorable details that help establish the themes of your story. Balance the use of details for emphasis. Do not overdo it; a scene can get buried in too much detail, obscuring the characters and the action. Report only the details that matter and are significant, and that reinforce the character(s), action(s), and theme(s) of your story.

Details in the Beginning, the Middle, and the End

Before you know the end of the story and the overall transformation the character undergoes, and before you have accomplished all of the above, writing details is premature. However, once you have made your way through several drafts and the overall dramatic action plot is energizing, the settings dazzling, and all the major scenes and turning points and energetic markers are supple, luminous, and amazing, turn your attention to making "every word perfect."

This is the fun part, or at least this step is a favorite of mine. You consider and develop the nuance of words and phrases, the atmosphere, a sense of mystery, irony, humor, symbolism, satire, mood, rhythm, presence, timeliness, beauty, or harmony.

The details in scenes in the beginning quarter of a story bring into sharp focus the objects the protagonist most identifies with. These objects often reflect her conditioning by her environment, upbringing, and culture. They can include:

- Where a character lives
- The clothes she wears
- The car she drives
- What she keeps in her medicine cabinet
- The contents of her refrigerator
- Her makeup bag
- Her choice of pictures for the walls of her apartment, town-house, or mansion

All these things constitute aspects of her ordinary world. They are externalizations of the character's inner life and convey meaning. In the beginning quarter of the story, the details you relay reflect the character as she is starting the story.

The mystery writer Raymond Chandler was a master of details. His stories, set in the sun-drenched, tawdry world of 1940s Los Angeles, rely on sharply observed details to convey in a sentence the essence of a character or setting. Consider the following:

> From thirty feet away she looked like a lot of class. From ten feet away she looked like something made up to be seen from thirty feet away.

> He looked about as inconspicuous as a tarantula on a slice of angel food cake.

> He snorted and hit me in the solar plexus. I bent over and took hold of the room with both hands and spun it. When I had it nicely spinning I gave it a full swing and hit myself on the back of the head with the floor.

Notice that in every one of these passages Chandler is *concrete* and *specific*. The details are the kind that you might notice (if you were very observant) and that give you particular clues to the characters and scenes they concern.

The details of a character's beginning world define whether she goes into the new world of the middle as a willing adventurer or resistant and full of pain caused by the loss of these objects. Unable to base her identity on her association with her possessions and lifestyle, she questions who she is. Thus begins her inner plot and the first step toward the incremental and ultimate character transformation.

When the protagonist moves out of the ordinary and conditioned world into an exotic and unknown world, the details shift to reflect who she is as she journeys into the great unknown.

The details she surrounds herself with at the end quarter of the story, and especially at the resolution, reveal the character's truth. Details—

hers and hers alone—deepen the reader's understanding of who the character is now and reflect her ultimate transformation.

PLOT WHISPER

Print out a hard copy of your novel, memoir, or screenplay and read every word with an analytical mind.

Now read a prize-winning novel in the same genre you are writing, by an author you admire. Take notes on the details the author uses to convey a fresh way of understanding the character's sensibilities and peel away the superficial to evoke the profound.

No word is extraneous in a story. Nothing is there simply because the language is beautiful, the action clever, or the character quirky. Every word contributes to the deeper meaning of the piece. How you treat the details of your story and choose to represent them becomes your own unique voice.

Scene Tracker for *The Great Gatsby* by F. Scott Fitzgerald
Thematic Significance Statement: Fascination with wealth, another man's wife, and old dreams is self-destructive.

Note: color-code names and descriptions, and keep each character's color consistent throughout. Use the Scene Tracker template from the Introduction.

Figure 10. Scene Tracker for the first few scenes of The Great Gatsby by F. Scott Fitzgerald

7 ESSENTIAL ELEMENTS OF SCENE

Chapter/Scene	Date & Setting	Character Emotional Development	Goal	Dramatic Action	Conflict	Emotional Change	Thematic Significance
Chpt 1, Scene 1	1924 summer; Long Island; East Egg	**Nick** late 20s; college to Army & now business life	have dinner w/Tom & Daisy	stroll around the estate	X	-/-/-	"2 young women buoyed up as though upon an anchored balloon" (shows insubstantiality & inner emptiness)
		Tom married to Daisy; enormously wealthy; a "cruel body"	Tom's scientific pursuits indicate his desire to preserve the status quo and foreshadows Gatsby's threat				
		Daisy 2nd cousin once removed; absurd, charming laugh; lonely since moving from Chicago; 2-yr-old daughter; lets others make her decisions					
		Jordan famous golfer					
Scene 2	same night, same place	**Jordan** tells Nick about Tom's infidelity		Nick learns about Tom	X	+/-	intro theme of adultery
		Daisy confesses her belief about her daughter					
Scene 3	same night, West Egg	**Gatsby** lives next door to Nick	go home	Gatsby trembling	X	+/-	Gatsby house is pretentious imitation of European structure; color green
Chpt 2, Scene 1	between West Egg & NY	**Tom** introduces Wilson & mistress	go to NY	husband present as Tom & mistress flirt	X	-/--	Valley of Ashes; gigantic, sightless eyes; dust & ashen veil

PART THREE

THE
JOURNEY

CHAPTER EIGHT
OPENING THE DOOR

Where you stumble and fall, there you will find gold.

—Joseph Campbell

The heart of the story begins the moment the protagonist steps away from her ordinary world and crosses into the exotic world. This movement across a threshold symbolizes the start of the journey. For readers to care about the journey (dramatic action plot), first they have to understand and care about who is doing what and why (character emotional development plot).

So far you have visualized, written, or charted on a plot planner the four energetic markers for your story. You know what your character wants and her reasons. You have identified what only your protagonist can do, deliver, conquer, or overcome. The fears, flaws, and strengths you give her make her believable and represent challenges she must overcome if she's to transform. She has a gift, though she will have to go through trials and challenges to reclaim it. You know why this is her story.

You have a list of themes and some details you plan to incorporate in your story. You have lined up formidable antagonists, each with goals in direct opposition to the protagonist's, ready to challenge her on her journey. You know where she has been and what her true journey and purpose are. You stand ready to catapult her into the very heart of the story world—the world of the middle.

But now, like your character, rather than surrender to the pull of the Universal Story and move into the great unknown, you find yourself dithering, reluctant to leave the safety of your ordinary world. To be the kind of writer who writes a story from the beginning to the end requires you to get serious. It's only natural to feel resistance as you leave your comfort zone. Getting through the middle portion of a story helps you replace resistance with acceptance. This isn't an easy task. As I'll explain, a death is involved.

To start, you need to understand the source of your fear, as well as your protagonist's reluctance to move into the middle of the journey. Fear is why writers spend inordinate amounts of time in the safety of the beginning one-quarter of the story.

PLOT WHISPER

Begin by exploring your protagonist's fear. Review the entry you wrote under "Fears" when you filled out the character profile for your protagonist. Revise and update it based on the knowledge and understanding of the character you've gained since.

As much as your protagonist wants to attain the goal you filled in the profile, she knows (or at least senses) the forces lining up to challenge her.

Review the list of antagonists you created. Are you using them to their maximum effect?

Another major stumbling block to moving into the middle part of the story is confusion about where the story should have begun in the first place.

The beginning of every great story reflects what comes at the end. This means you cannot determine what comes at the beginning until you know what happens at the end. T. S. Eliot said it best: "The end is in the beginning."

The beginning of any entertaining and well-crafted story foreshadows where the characters will be at the end. If you're going to successfully lay the groundwork for the character and show the plot building to a climax in a way that makes the crowning glory of the entire story seem both inevitable and surprising, you first need to know what happens at that climax. This means that *until you write the end you do not truly know the beginning*.

THE WRITER'S WAY

Now is the time to explore your fear and the source of your resistance. Review the fears you entered when filling in the writer's profile for yourself. Revise and update them.

As much as you want to write a worthy story from beginning to end (or the goal you stated in the profile), you know, or at least sense, the forces lining up to challenge you.

Review the list of antagonists you created for yourself. Now that you know what they represent, try to see them as teachers who will help you become a better writer and a stronger, more confident person.

As you create more conflict, tension, and suspense in your protagonist's life, suppress your personal antagonists as much as possible and resolve distractions as quickly as you can in your writing life.

What Should You Do?

Do you labor over the first three-quarters of a project in which the groundwork is laid for the end? Or, do you write the climax first?

My solution is to begin anywhere. Just start. Do whatever you must to write an entire draft all the way through to the end, including the climax. One completed draft of your story gives you an advantage: you know the end of the story.

If you find the courage to not only begin writing but to continue, you'll discover that the energy of the Universal Story does not cease at thresholds. Instead, the energy of your story, of your life, of your world, heightens. The longer you dally at any barrier, the longer it takes to achieve your dreams. Thrust yourself forward. Send the protagonist on her way. You are not alone. The Universal Story will assist you.

The Protagonist Crosses the Threshold

Some thresholds are portals or grand entrances to a new and different world. Alice goes down the rabbit hole into a world where door mice talk and a pack of playing cards holds trial. Harry runs from the world, of the Muggles straight through a seemingly solid barrier and onto a train platform where the Hogwarts Express prepares to depart. Characters can cross a bridge, plunge into a forest, journey through space and time, or ride the eye of a tornado. It's a passage that takes one moment or forever.

Every step in every quest involves a separation; the initiate leaves what is comfortable, familiar, and ordinary and enters the unknown. The tree seed breaks through the surface of the earth, the fetus leaves the mother's womb, a caterpillar emerges from the cocoon.

Often these thresholds are guarded. The significance of the threshold in the story determines the power of the threshold guardian(s). Gatekeepers guard the passage both ways. In classical mythology, the gateway to the Underworld was guarded by Cerberus, a fierce three-headed dog.

Sometimes the challenge is not a physical guardian, but a barrier presented by the threshold itself. In Lewis Carroll's classic, Alice can't find a door she can fit through—she's either too big or too small. In *Harry Potter and the Sorcerer's Stone*, Harry struggles to locate the gate that's magically hidden in King's Cross Station. Like any antagonist, a threshold guardian can be another character, nature, machine, society, or a false belief. Always it embodies at least a touch of fear. Even before Harry embarks on the train ride toward his new life, he finds himself incapable of finding the train platform. A passing guard starts to get annoyed at his persistent questions about Platform 9¾—a site that doesn't exist. Harry's mouth turns dry. He begins to feel desperate. A large clock over the arrivals board keeps the reader focused on how little time Harry has to discover the doorway to his train. The minute hand ticks nearer and nearer to the train's departure time from a gate both Harry and the reader are beginning to worry he'll never find.

Thresholds as Transitions

Thresholds serve as transitions from one scene to another. The decision to show a character crossing a threshold in a scene or to tell it in summary depends on the threshold's importance to the overall story.

A threshold's significance is defined by the importance of the scene the protagonist is moving into. In other words, if your protagonist is simply moving across the front door threshold after a day at work and into her private life, a simple line of transition is enough. If, however, your protagonist is moving across the front door threshold well aware that a stalker awaits her on the other side and that by doing so she burns all bridges, the moment of crossing becomes paramount and thus is shown moment-by-moment in scene. (In this example, I am using a door threshold to represent a literary/plot threshold. Keep in mind, every actual door a character goes through does not automatically signify that the story is moving to a different plane.)

Every threshold your protagonist crosses from one symbolic place to another has the potential to alert the reader and the audience that the character is transitioning from the known to the unknown. Excitement builds.

At the start of the middle of *To Kill a Mockingbird*, Harper Lee writes that Scout wakes up to snow, something she has never seen before. Scout screams, "The world's endin', Atticus!" Lee's use of snow here and Scout's reaction to it foreshadows the change that is coming, her entrance into a new and unusual world.

Scout's world as she knows it ends after she is "so busy looking at the fire you didn't know it when [Boo] put the blanket around you." The moment Scout understands Boo is not the "malevolent phantom" she imagined during the beginning of the book she is pushed over the threshold into an exotic world where the story turns. In this new world, all Scout's beliefs will be challenged and the demands on her from family and friends will take on more significance and seriousness.

But before that lies the threshold where she watches a poignant part of her childhood burn to the ground.

Thresholds create suspense. Until the protagonist takes action, excitement grips the reader.

Will she go forward as she planned, decided, or was persuaded to do? Or will she stay stuck? Or, through a plot twist, will she not go back to the old or forward to the expected, but instead turn somewhere else entirely?

Thresholds Hold Tension

Thresholds, such as Dorothy's tornado or Alice's rabbit hole or Harry's train ride, take ordinary characters into an exotic realm soaked in mystery. Air, water, and fire can create high energetic swirling spots in your story. When the protagonist departs the ordinary world, without the reader knowing where she is going to end up, tension and suspense result.

Anticipation creates emotion in your story and emotion creates reader participation.

Think of a threshold as the anticipatory phase. After the character reacts to the dramatic action and before the next dramatic action looms a gap of anticipation. Everyone—the writer and the audience as well as the character—viscerally feels the moment of anticipation. What is going to happen?

Often, the anticipation of some event is worse than the actual event itself.

In the beginning of *The Old Man and the Sea*, Ernest Hemingway sets up the protagonist's dilemma. An old Cuban fisherman has not caught fish for so long he is now deemed unlucky by all the other fishermen and the boy he loves is no longer permitted to fish with him. The old man desperately wants to live up to the boy's image of him as the greatest fisherman of all time.

The threshold separating the old world—going out to fish like every other day—and the new world—finding fish—begins with the arrival of a man-of-war bird. The bird heralds fish as it circles above the sea. Then come dolphins.

> Another and another rose and they were jumping in all directions, churning the water and leaping in long jumps after the bait. They were circling it and driving it.

For seven pages in this novella, the old man travels between the world of catching no fish and the world of catching the largest fish he has ever seen in his long life. Each new symbol of the world to come builds greater anticipation as the dolphins drive the bait and pull the old man toward his destiny.

A major stumbling block constitutes one kind of threshold. At the end of the first quarter of *The Grapes of Wrath* Grampa says, "I jus' ain't a-going'." Conniving a way to force him to go to California, the rest of his family carries Grampa to the truck together and, as a family, they cross the threshold from their ruined homestead in Oklahoma toward the promised land.

In the Newbery Medal–winning book *Hatchet* by Gary Paulsen, thirteen-year-old Brian Robeson travels by plane from his childhood home to visit his father in a remote area in Alaska. At the end of the beginning of the story, the pilot of the private plane and the only other person aboard suffers a fatal heart attack. As the plane crash-lands, Brian is sent far from his ordinary world of being safely supported by adults into the wilderness alone with nothing but a hatchet and his own wits to save him.

At each threshold, the Universal Story makes the decision for the protagonist. She cannot go back. She has to go forward.

PLOT WHISPER

Between leaving behind the introductory world of the Universal Story, energetic markers, plot planners, character profiles, and theme, and before entering the middle of writing a draft all the way to the end, purge all extraneous notes. Tidy up your workspace and organize yourself.

- Hang your plot planner where you will see or pass it often throughout the day.

- Keep a stack of colored sticky notes and pencils or pens nearby.

- Fill in the beginning section of the plot planner from the first scene to the end of the beginning scene. Choose the appropriate sticky note color—one each for the character emotional development plot, the dramatic action plot, and any thematic elements for each scene.

- Plot dramatic action scenes in the beginning, where an antagonist is in control, above the line on a plot planner using the appropriate dramatic action plot sticky note color. Write the effect the antagonist's external actions have on the protagonist on the correct colored sticky notes for the character emotional development plot.

- Scenes where an antagonist holds the power over the protagonist create more energy than do scenes where the protagonist is safe and calm. Place these scenes above the plot planner line, as they keep the story moving. Plot the scenes in which the protagonist is in charge below the line. These slow the story.

- Stand back. Determine the flow of energy between the protagonist and the antagonist(s) at the beginning of your story. Where and how does the energy surge? Assess the flow of energy in all the scenes in order to evaluate your story's overall intensity level.

- Purchase a calendar for the year to devote to your writing. Mark on the calendar the day you plan to finish this draft of your story.

- Assess what you have accomplished thus far in your story and determine the total number of pages you need to finish in order to reach the end. Multiple by 250 for the total number of words necessary to tell your story (250 words per page). Divide that by the number of writing days between your goal date and today.

- Work your way backward on the calendar to determine how many words you need to write every writing day and approximately how much time you need to allocate to each session. You may find that to accomplish your goal you have to wake an hour earlier or stay up an hour later than you currently do. You might have to limit commitments and daily-life obligations in order to put yourself and your writing first.

- Schedule your writing days and times in pen on your calendar. Dreams never leave. They hound, haunt, whisper, and beckon you closer to what you most fear. It is easy to quit. But to reach that which you long for most, the treasure you seek, you first must face your greatest fear.

You may think:
- It's a lot of work.
- My family might not like it.
- I could fail.
- I'll expose myself to ridicule.
- I'm not smart enough.
- I'm not good enough.
- I'm not . . .

THE WRITER'S WAY

The jewel of the Universal Story lies in each forward step. You move deeper until you stand on the threshold of a major turning point in your life. Words demand to be written. If they are not expressed by you, they go unsaid.

The moment you are convinced you cannot go forward is precisely the moment to forge ahead. The depth of your fear and resistance determines the potential for profound change. Leave behind old beliefs and take with you the promise of something new.

Cross from your normal, regular life over the threshold into your writing life and sacred space. You know what this moment represents in the Universal Story. Consciously turn the energy to your benefit.

Finding the New Place and the Protagonist's Place in It

As in real life, in stories when one door closes another opens. The protagonist enters a new world, be it a new physical place or a new psychological state. This new world offers the opportunity to evolve and be transformed.

The middle of a story focuses on goals and dreams. The protagonist carries her goals as she steps into the middle and the actual story world itself. She may enter the middle of the story with the same goal(s) with which she began the story. Or, because of all she experiences in the beginning, she changes or refines her goals before moving forward into the unknown world.

In *The Old Man and the Sea*, the fisherman begins the story with a goal of going out far to sea, only hoping to be lucky enough to catch anything and with absolutely no illusions of topping his record fish of eighty-seven pounds. Then, based on the signs given the fisherman in the threshold between the two worlds, he refines his goal of catching just anything to ". . . think of only one thing. That which I was born for. There might be a big one around that school, he thought."

In order to reach these new goals, the protagonist first must learn new skills, many of which may be present already but undiscovered, underdeveloped, or forgotten.

The challenges in the middle strip away the protagonist's personal power, will, and autonomy. They tear apart beliefs, reveal judgments, and force self-confrontation, all of which serve the ultimate transformation at the end.

In *The Daily Coyote*, a best-selling memoir by Shreve Stockton, a newly transplanted twenty-something city girl alone in the country for the first time enters the world of the middle of the story when she agrees to adopt a ten-day-old orphaned coyote whom she names Charlie. Each month of Charlie's life represents progressively challenging trials. Shreve struggles as she deepens her understanding of her surroundings and environment. Charlie also matures, and Stockton's tension between what it means to be wild and what's possible to be tamed escalates to threaten her very life.

You Can't Go Home Again

As the protagonist moves deeper into the new world, emotions she has suppressed and therefore never processed begin to well up and unravel her self-control. Unable to function at a superficial level any longer, she begins to truly feel. The more she is prevented from reaching her goal, the more emotions she experiences. Now, she not only has to acknowledge her feelings but actually feel them, too. Only then can she learn from her feelings and grow to trust them and herself.

In the middle of a story, emotion rises for the audience as well.

Most of us live the same story over and over again. If we are brave enough to move away from everything we know (end of the beginning), by the time things start to get messy—which they must in the middle—we, too, often give up, turn a blind eye, and stick our heads in the sand. We end up back "home," licking our wounds.

In stories, once the protagonist advances into the middle of the story, she does not have the option of turning back. Moving ever deeper into the exotic world, she begins to understand more of the rules of this new world and her place in it. If she looks back at the ordinary world, she feels guilt, regret, resentment, grievances, sadness, bitterness, and blame. You may be doing that yourself right now. Think of all the time you procrastinated in the past because of fear and insecurity about your ability to create a masterpiece.

Recommitment Scene

Throughout all the drama in the middle, the Universal Story sends a bright and steady beacon of light. Exactly in the middle of the middle stands the second energetic marker. Reach it and recommit. When the protagonist most wants to run the other way, this is the precise moment for your protagonist and for you to forge ahead instead.

In the middle of the memoir, *Farm City*, Novella Carpenter is faced with the loss of two of her neighbors. One neighbor, who is responsible for Carpenter's decision to live by a plot of land on which she has created a farm in the heart of a downtown Oakland ghetto, moves away of her own accord. The other neighbor, Bobby, who lives in an immobilized car with a television mounted on top of another abandoned car on the dead-end street, and who keeps her company with his salute and toothless grin, is hauled away in a police car and his entire world is carried off by a tow truck.

By now, Novella has learned the rules of this exotic world she lives in and has begun to create an oasis in the desert. So, when faced with loss, rather than give up, Novella recommits to the adventure by pledging to eat exclusively from her July garden. She wants to prove to herself that she is a real farmer, capable of feeding herself completely off her own fruits, vegetables, and livestock for an entire month.

THE WRITER'S WAY

The halfway point challenges the writer's resistance. At one of my workshops, two writers in two days both battled what could very well be the most common cause of resistance and the deadliest of all writers' antagonists: the internal critic. You know when this overzealous critic struts in because the creative process skids to a halt. A voice in your head discounts your efforts and belittles your writing. Criticisms about your story clutter your mind: it's not good enough or witty enough or profound enough. Nattering doubts grow. All of this negativity sends your energy plummeting. This critic is known to act up especially at major thresholds. As if on a teeter-totter, you slide between the fear of going forward into the unknown and the urge to go back and start again. You begin to separate from your story. The vision dims.

When you arrive at a threshold, do not go back and relive old familiar territory. Stand up for your story. You are being tested. Take a moment. Give thanks for all you have written. Restate your goals. Commit to reaching the end of the draft. Seal the commitment with a conscious act that signifies you have burned all bridges. The only way is forward.

Appreciate that the right words do not always come out the first time. You cannot always convey what you imagine for your story the first, second, third, or even fourth try. Writing is a process. Get the words down. Later you can go back and be brilliant.

Conflict Leading to Self-Discovery

Andre Agassi, international tennis star, says he despised tennis from the start. He writes in his memoir, *Open: An Autobiography*, that in the middle of his journey to wholeness he quit drugs and alcohol and committed to tennis for the very first time.

Agassi's halfway point does what all good halfway points do: signals a move away from ambivalence to commitment. Having truly committed, he assumes his fate will improve, that his reward for recommitting is success, and he is near to attaining his goal. However, as most of us—as well as our characters—discover, Agassi quickly finds that rather than things getting better, the halfway point signals they are about to get worse. The fear he attempted to numb with drugs and alcohol has nowhere to hide. His demons confront him head-on.

After your protagonist recommits to her goal(s) at the halfway point of the Universal Story, she feels the energy in her life rise in significance. This energetic surge is a warning to the reader. Wake up. Be alert. A crisis is coming.

Believing she is in control now that she is fully committed to the journey, the protagonist moves with confidence deeper into the Universal Story and makes what she thinks is the final push forward. She is no longer afraid of how she goes about ensuring her success and is willing to use any and all strategies at her disposal.

To help decide the direction and movement of the story, writers employ as many of the following as needed, at both the scene level and overall story level. These give the story substance and detail, reveal more about who the character truly is, and deepen the conflict, tension, suspense, or curiosity of the story in the middle.

- Conspiracy
- Authority
- Aggression
- Deception
- Rescue
- Mistaken identity
- False affection
- Criminal action
- Suspicion
- Dishonor

As the energy rises and her defenses fall away, the character opens up more and more to the reader. The more vulnerable she becomes, the more the protagonist reveals who she really is. Life gets harder, but little does she know just how much more difficult things are going to become.

Powerful antagonists leap in, and she quickly finds herself under siege, pummeled by forces intent on preventing her success. The energy of the story fills with more conflict, tension, suspense, and/or curiosity in every scene.

The shifting of power back and forth between the protagonist and the antagonist now slams all the way to the antagonist's advantage and stays there. Self-doubt and uncertainty begin to smother the protagonist. She struggles with shortcomings. Yet she also discovers strengths she did not know she possessed. The protagonist becomes more and more conscious of her thoughts, feelings, and actions, and sees her life differently. Any joy she experiences in success is best modulated—if she thinks her victory constitutes a sign that conquest is near, she quickly finds herself mistaken and it becomes incumbent upon her to re-evaluate the situation. No route forward is without its dangers and peril.

Early in the middle of a story, the energy of the character emotional development plot and the dramatic action plot often flattens out as the exotic world develops. After the recommitment scene in the middle of the middle, the line of the plot planner begins to build in earnest, climbing steadily higher. This indicates the need to methodically build the story energy through the use of conflict, tension, and suspense.

In John Steinbeck's *East of Eden*, the protagonist, Cal, struggles with the darkness of the truth he is surrounded by in the middle of the novel. His mother is not dead. She is running a whorehouse in downtown Salinas, and his greatest fear is that he is bad like she is. At the halfway point of the story, Cal sees his mother for the first time. When he decides, "I've got her in me but I don't have to be like her," he finds in himself the strength to commit to try to be good. At that point, the true battle between good and evil begins.

The protagonist grows alarmed and bewildered, angry and hateful, jealous and envious, fearful and sad. She exhibits these negative emotions as the confrontations by the antagonists become more vigorous and tumultuous. The character's flaws that were merely introduced earlier are revealed now in the full scope of dysfunction. If she was shown as controlling in the beginning, we now see when she is threatened to what lengths she is willing to go in order to regain control. If she was shown as fearful, we now see how deep that fear runs.

PLOT WHISPER

Put all scenes building to the crisis above the plot planner line. Create more conflict by immersing the protagonist in situations where she is not in control, where she is faced with her greatest fear and with what she most hates, with treachery and opposition.

Rip all power from the protagonist and transfer it to the antagonist. Make the dramatic action a contest of searing intensity between the two. Threaten the protagonist with more tension and disruption in each scene. Put her under more strain and stress in each progressive scene. The more she denies and becomes exasperated and overwhelmed, the greater her resistance and the more she struggles.

As the energy of the story builds, the protagonist becomes painfully aware of an almost continuous undercurrent of low-level unease and restlessness, boredom and nervousness. She feels anxious, fearful of something looming and ready to strike. Her best behavior long gone, she passes judgments. Negative emotions grow within her. She resents, resists, and denies.

The protagonist, of course, is not aware the antagonists mirror her own dysfunction. Instead, she sees imperfection only in others. Hot emotions escape from beneath the surface. She reacts with anger, fear, aggression, and depression. She attacks, argues, judges, and blames with jealousy, wanting control. Often she withdraws, hostile and seeking revenge.

All along and deep down throughout the middle, the story is building to a crisis. The reader tastes it, senses it, and feels it coming. She tries to pretend nothing bad is about to happen, but there is no denying the inevitable. Doom is about to strike. There is no other way for the story to go.

On some level, the character knows it too. Emotions intensify as the energy of the story rises.

CHAPTER NINE

THE MIDDLE OF THE JOURNEY

I'm not a very good writer, but I'm an excellent rewriter.

—James Michener

The primary plot is the plot thread that defines the direction of your story as either an outer journey the protagonist takes or an inner journey by the protagonist. To determine your primary plot, ask yourself whether you lean more toward developing dramatic action or character reactions. Do you enjoy writing about motion or emotion? Are you more interested in what the protagonist is out to attain or what she ultimately will become? The answers to these questions define the primary plot. They also tend to define you as a left-brained or right-brained writer. One type isn't superior to the other; they're just different.

All other plot lines developed for a story—romance, mystery, political, historical—are subplots. Subplots tie to and reinforce the primary plot; they predominate in the middle.

Using Subplots to Develop the Protagonist's Flaws

The progression of the protagonist's internal flaw or character emotional development plot often serves as a subplot to a dramatic action-driven story in which the primary plot revolves around external action.

155

The dramatic action demands a goal. The character emotional development demands growth.

The protagonist's internal conflict or fatal flaw reveals what she needs to achieve internally in order to gain the goal of the primary plot. The resolution of the primary plot is dependent upon the resolution of the internal subplot.

SUBPLOTS IN THE MIDDLE

The middle of a story often has a subplot(s) of its own. This subplot contains a beginning (as the character leaves her ordinary world and enters the exotic world) that leads to a middle. A rise in intensity often corresponds with the second energetic marker of the overall story's primary plot when the protagonist commits to the journey. A subplot that lasts only as long as the middle culminates energetically just before the third energetic marker of the primary plot's crisis. (Do not confuse a crisis with the climax. The climax comes at the end of the overall story itself and shows the character fully in her own personal power. The crisis shows the protagonist at her worst—after all, it is a crisis.)

EXAMPLES OF SUBPLOTS

The middle-grade novel *The Cay* by Theodore Taylor has a clearly identifiable subplot with a beginning, middle, and end running through the middle of the overall story. This subplot includes the four energetic markers, though the subplot begins and ends in the middle. The subplot in the middle of *The Cay* is like its own short, short story, while also contributing dramatically to the protagonist's emotional development in the overall story.

The story is concerned with a young boy's attempt to escape the island of Curacao during World War II in order to return to his home in Virginia. In the escape attempt, he is stranded after a shipwreck on an island with a black man named Timothy and a cat for companions. At the first energetic marker of the story, the boy, Phillip, awakens blinded from the accident and thrust into a world of darkness bereft of both his parents. The antagonists in the exotic world of the island are

Phillip's prejudice of against Timothy because of his race, blindness, the island itself, fear of never being able to see again, fear of never being reunited with his mother and father, fear of living his entire life on the island, feeling sorry for himself, the weather, and malaria. Phillip's allies in the middle of the story are Timothy and Stew Cat.

Phillip's goal could be viewed as threefold: to survive, to get his sight back, and to be rescued. All of these require either the help of others or a miracle. In other words, none of his goals are within his own power to achieve without help, which makes them not true goals but rather dreams/desires. In the beginning of many coming-of-age stories, the major choices in the protagonist's journey are made by the adults in his life. Maturation and the growth of the child's own power occur when the child is left to rely completely on himself. Phillip moves through the story without a concrete, tangible goal until the tiny, though significant subplot in the middle of the story.

In the middle of *The Cay*, Timothy makes the two of them a camp, sets up a fire as a signal beacon, and arranges rocks to spell out "Help." He catches fish for them to eat, while telling Phillip that above them, forty feet from the ground, is a feast of "big, fat green coconuts." Timothy is too old to climb the palm tree, and Phillip is too scared. All of these action scenes mark the beginning of the subplot and show Phillip in his ordinary initial state on the island: mostly helpless and often scared.

After a month and a half on the island, and after having saved Timothy's life and learned to fish, Phillip is finally ready to climb the palm tree. The moment he wraps his arms around the tree trunk and begins to climb, he enters the exotic world of the middle of the subplot.

At the insistence of Timothy, Phillip grudgingly maneuvers himself through a survival course, designed to help him come to terms with his blindness in the exotic world of living on an island. When he begins to climb the palm tree, Phillip ascends about ten feet, freezes with fear, and climbs down. This moment, when Phillip feels he has let down his mentor, also serves as the character emotional development crisis. Often, if the character emotional development is a subplot, its crisis is not at the same point in the same scene as the crisis in the dramatic action primary plot, which occurs toward the end of the middle. Instead, one will hit here at the middle of the middle and the other at the customary three-quarters of the way through the entire story. This is what happens in *The Cay*. Phillip's personal crisis point and the highest energy in the story so far occurs about halfway through the entire story, when he fails in his attempt to climb the palm tree.

The climax of the survival subplot on the island happens when Phillip attempts the climb again, makes it to the top, picks two coconuts, and returns safely. He asks Timothy, "Are you still black?" showing Phillip has both overcome his fear and his prejudice. Phillip's reaction to his successful climb shows his recommitment to the adventure—in this case, survival. This entire episode constitutes one of the novel's subplots and plays a major role in Phillip's character emotional development plot.

In *The Cay*, the crisis for the primary dramatic action plot of the overall story comes at exactly the three-quarter mark when a hurricane hits the island. But as we've seen, the crisis of the subplot comes much earlier.

In *To Kill a Mockingbird* by Harper Lee, the primary plot dealing with Boo breaks off after the end of the beginning scene and rarely reappears in either name or physical presence until the final quarter of the entire story and end of the primary plot. The middle is made up of almost independent yet complementary subplots until the last quarter, when the primary plot links back to the first-quarter plot that includes Boo. The primary plot is really about Scout coming of age, and every subplot in the middle contributes to that. Yet the relationship between Scout and Boo is primary in that Boo symbolically represents Scout's character emotional development plot. Yes, thanks to the subplots of the middle, Scout learns from her aunt how to be a lady and from the trial, where her father represents Tom Robinson, about life in general. Both episodes contribute to Scout's overall emotional development, but it is her interactions with her strange neighbor that constitutes the primary plot of the story.

When the dramatic action primary plot line dealing with Boo breaks off after the first quarter of the story at the end of the beginning, a subplot begins in which Scout must first learn to control herself and then not to fight. At the same time, she is also asked to mature and to develop empathy for others. Typically, in most coming-of-age stories, the character starts the story with a flaw, whether immaturity, ignorance, fear, or innocence, and acquires mastery over it by the novel's end.

In the middle of the story, when angry farmers show up at the jail and threaten Atticus, Scout steps forward, embodying all the lessons she has learned in the middle of the story: to walk in another person's shoes. She shows mastery over herself and her ability to save the day in a way she could not have done in any other part of the story so far. This represents Scout's recommitment scene.

Goal Setting

Goal setting plays a big part in the development of the overall dramatic action plot of your story. It's also important to establish goal setting in every scene. Short-term goals are specific tasks, objectives, or actions your character determines will take her nearer to accomplishing her long-term goal within a clearly defined period of time.

One technique to create depth in a story is to provide several thematically tied goals throughout the story—a romantic goal, a mystery goal, a personal goal, a political goal, a dramatic action goal, etc. Each of these creates a subplot.

Cara Black, in her murder mystery series set in Parisian neighborhoods, joins the two best-selling genres today: mystery and romance. In *Murder in Montmartre*, Aimee, the protagonist, has an overall story goal to prove her friend did not kill her partner and thus to absolve her of the crime. Aimee also has a personal goal to solve: a mystery about her father. Both goals help keep her focused on the task at hand, even when the energy is at its highest and the action at the most dangerous.

Dreams or desires add yet another layer. Because dreams generally rely on the help of others or a bit of magic, they often create an added twist at the end of the story.

At the beginning of *Murder in Montmartre*, Aimee's boyfriend breaks up with her. Throughout the story we feel Aimee's loneliness, and how much she misses her beau and longs for love; this sets up her romance goal. Thus, when she unexpectedly finds a man who excites her passion, the story takes on added depth and excitement. For Aimee, finding love and achieving her dream is an added bonus. The reader is excited about reading the next book in the series to learn if the two lovers will last as a couple.

If the character's story goal is at odds with her dream they cannot both come true. There will be a conflict that must be resolved in the story.

A dream for your characters (and for you, too) is a just a dream . . . until the character takes an active step toward realizing it. Then it becomes a goal.

Scene Tracker for *Murder in Montmartre* by Cara Black

Thematic Significance Statement: To live in the here and now and continue a journey, one must put the ghosts to rest.

Figure 11. Scene Tracker for Cara Black's *Murder in Montmartre*

ESSENTIAL ELEMENTS OF SCENE

Chpt/Scene	Date & Setting	Character Emotional Development	Goal	Dramatic Action	Conflict	Emotional Change	Thematic Significance
Chpt 1, Scene 1	Paris, 1995, January, Snowy Monday night	Aimee Leduc: she's late; never rely on a guy or let him know you do; Dog: Miles Davis	Stop boyfriend from leaving her	Break up	X	Pensive changes to scared changes to angry	Ghosts used in 3rd line
End of the Beginning	The next morning	Aimee: doesn't take no for an answer; persistent; goes the distance for a friend	Wants the police report	Learns her friend will be charged with the murder	X	Determined changes to scared changes to angry	
Middle	4 nights later, Thursday late evening	Aimee: brazen in the face of danger	Escape the bad guy	On the run; stranger protects her; only time she relies on someone else—she likes it	X	Fear changes to curiosity changes to fear	
The End	Friday night, deserted hospital	Aimee: has figured out where the killers are; musician and Aimee kiss	Find killers	Falls into an old quarry; gun at her head; boyfriend tied up; fight to the finish; gets the killer	Highest in the entire story	Fear turns to strength	Aimee crawls on all fours in white gypsum; "You look like a ghost."

The Crisis: The Biggest Challenge to the Protagonist

The crisis is an event in a written scene that works like any crisis in real life. It shakes things up in such a way that the protagonist must act. The crisis takes on dramatic proportions when it serves as the highest point in the dramatic action plot line so far. At the same time, the crisis forces the protagonist to rethink life. This wake-up call in turn changes her character emotional development. When one scene impacts both action and emotional plotlines in such a dramatic way, the scene acquires a lot of power and importance. This effect can generally be found toward the end of the middle or nearly three-quarters of the way through the project.

For instance, at the end of the middle in *To Kill a Mockingbird*, the jury for Tom Robinson's trial reconvenes to announce its verdict to the judge, Atticus, and the rest of the courtroom. This high point in both the dramatic action and the character emotional development plots is not loud and violent; rather, we see it almost in slow motion and from far away. Paradoxically, this creates even more impact. Scout's confidence that the jury will do the right thing quickly turns to shock as the jurors avert their eyes from the defendant.

Hearing the guilty verdict shakes both the protagonist, Scout, and her brother, Jem, at their cores. In the moment the verdict is rendered, Scout's innocence and belief in the essential goodness of the world are stripped away. She is left struggling to make sense of things.

The Crisis Represented on a Plot Planner

Readers and audiences expect and deserve the dramatic action and the character emotional development to build to a fevered pitch toward the end of the middle of the entire story. As the examples above demonstrate, the crisis scene(s) can be written softly or violently.

At the crisis of *The Lord of the Flies*, the antagonist, Jack, is fully in his power after having killed and roasted a pig. He threatens Ralph with violence, demanding to know from the others who will join his tribe and make him chief over Ralph. Amid exploding thunder and big drops of rain, Ralph attempts to draw the others to his side. "A wave of restlessness set the boys swaying and moving aimlessly." Jack seizes on the boys' hesitation and unites them in a dance, chanting, "Kill the beast! Cut his throat! Spill his blood!" In a frenzy of fear and excitement, all the boys turn on what they believe is the beast. The death is shown in moment-by-moment clarity as the boys "screamed, struck, bit, tore. There were no words, and no movements but the tearing of teeth and claws."

Either way, after enduring tension building throughout the middle, readers and audiences deserve a release. The crisis provides that.

The crisis is the lowest point in the entire story for the protagonist. However, at that point, the energy of the Universal Story is at its highest.

The plot planner is drawn the way it is because:

1. It replicates the energy of the Universal Story.
2. It differentiates the most important threshold in the entire story that comes directly after the crisis.
3. It shows the moment, when the fully conscious protagonist takes the first step toward the completion of her final goal and the true ending of the story begins.

Stored-up energy from the friction between the protagonist and antagonists increases throughout the middle of a story. Emotions such as unease, discontentment, boredom, and moodiness turn acute in the protagonist. As well, stronger emotions such as fear, uncertainty, resentment, resistance, bitterness, indignation, aggravation, and offense intensify. The reader can see the protagonist's normal faults and flaws become even more exaggerated. Hostile forces reach the tensest point of opposition. Separated, stretched too far, held too tightly, allowed too little by herself, by others, by her circumstances, or all of the above, the protagonist reaches her limit.

At the crisis of *East of Eden*, Cal's father rejects Cal. At the crisis of *Lord of the Flies*, the boys beat one of their own to death. Francesca falls in love with the traveling photographer at the crisis of *The Bridges of Madison County* by Robert James Waller. At the crisis of Deborah Santana's memoir, *Space Between the Stars*, she learns about her husband's infidelity. A hurricane causes a flood and a deadly snake bites Tea Cake at the crisis of *Their Eyes Were Watching God* by Zora Neale Hurston. All of these show the extent to which the protagonist is tested by events, whether internal or external.

FACING DEATH OR WORSE

A major challenge, threat, or loss in the protagonist's life situation (whether real or imagined), or a conflict in a relationship causes a complete rupture between who the protagonist has always been and who she is destined to be. The tear comes from deep within her and thematically symbolizes the cracking apart of her past identity.

The sudden release of energy in the crisis knocks the protagonist to her knees. At the crisis, the protagonist becomes conscious of who she truly is. In that new awareness, her old self dies and a new self is born.

A disaster, catastrophe, emergency, calamity, major predicament, or crisis of any kind qualifies as the protagonist's darkest hour. Failure, brokenness, fear, emptiness, alienation, and suffering a great loss reveal the true road. An emotionally significant event or radical change of status in the protagonist's life leads to death. Death leads the way to re-creation.

The crisis is the point in a sequence of scenes where the trend of all future events, for better or for worse, is determined. Occurring at the third energetic marker, it is the key turning point in your story.

In the novel *The Secret Life of Bees* by Sue Monk Kidd (and screenplay of the same name by Gina Prince-Bythewood), the young protagonist, Lily, is finally ready, around three-quarters of the way through the story, to tell August, the woman who has become like a mother to her, about her real mother. In this scene, all of Lily's worst fears are realized when August tells her that after Lily's birth her mother suffered a nervous breakdown. Leaving Lily behind, she came to live with August who had been her family's housekeeper. Lily turns angry and bitter about her mother's abandonment and leaving her on the peach farm with her neglectful and abusive father though beneath the surface emotions lies the devastating fear that she is responsible for killing her own mother when her mother finally did come back for her. This scene works as the highest point in the story and is quickly followed by a scene that takes the energy of the story even higher in terms of Lily's character emotional development. By exposing her secrets to the light, she transforms herself; she will never be the same.

After Lily and August talk, Lily displays the full measure of her pain and anger as she destroys the honey room, smashing hundreds of mason jars of honey. Here, Lily surrenders completely to her old personality. In the threshold scene that follows, and alarmed by her searing and destructive power, Lily acknowledges a shift in her consciousness. Newly awakened, she knows she must never again surrender to her anger.

I cannot stress this enough. The crisis scene represents the end of something, a death (figuratively, symbolically, or metaphorically) of a job, a relationship, a belief, or an old personality. This is an all-is-lost moment where tension and conflict peak. A crisis is a deep disappointment, a blow, the dark night of the soul. A crisis heralds the full transformation at the end of the story, but first comes a severing from the past, and at the crisis the protagonist suffers.

The crisis is a breakdown with the potential for a breakthrough.

THE ENERGETIC INTENSITY OF THE CRISIS

The degree of the rupture's violence and explosiveness is in direct proportion to the story genre. A suspenseful, high-action, thrilling story demands high intensity. A dramatic-action story releases quite a bit more obvious physical energy than does a quieter, slower, and more internal character-driven story.

Whether the crisis represents an emotional or circumstantial upheaval in the character's life, it releases the reader's fatigue and frustration and creates unbearable tension for the character and the reader.

A crisis forces the character to let go, detach, surrender, do things differently, get control of her life, and believe in herself.

THE WRITER'S WAY

Writers typically reach a crisis point about three-quarters of the way through writing a novel, memoir, or screenplay. Plot lines turn into a jumbled mass. You feel ready to cry and throw up your hands. Deep creases on either side of your mouth sag all the way down to your chin. You moan to yourself, "Nothing fits."

Look at the crisis of your story. Look for thematic significance in the details used in this scene of highest energetic intensity. For instance, in a fury of frustration the protagonist throws a valuable mirror to the floor. Ask yourself: Why the mirror? What thematic significance does the mirror have? Ask yourself how the character's flaw contributes to the crisis. When you find yourself with no answers, you have several choices. Knowing what you now know about your own internal antagonists, which choice do you make about your writing?

You know from critique group feedback that your crisis does not work—or the realization has slowly been dawning on you while reading through this book. Do you relinquish your power and surrender your will to an authority outside of yourself? A story is about the protagonist reclaiming her own personal power. The same thing applies to you on your writer's journey.

Perhaps at this point you shout that you don't get it. Chances are the lament that follows replicates exactly what you have been reading about "the crisis." You are overwhelmed by the new world you entered when you started reading this book. Each of the exercises you've encountered in this book tests you, just as your protagonist is tested throughout the middle of her journey.

Your despair is wrenching. Now you are approaching your crisis on a purely emotional level. You need to come to grips with it on an intellectual level, as well. This knowing has not traveled deeply enough for you to fully accept the input and willingly give up what you have imagined and written.

Your denial quickly turns to anger. To dissipate the negative energy, suggest to yourself that you are fine. Your story is fine. Encourage yourself not to give over your power and authority to the concepts offered here in this book.

By now red rims have formed around your bloodshot eyes as you move through the stages of grief. Take a deep breath. As oxygen reaches your lungs, you shudder.

Having reached a breaking point, out of a multitude of choices, you have fallen into victimization—a fatal flaw. You have relinquished your power, believing you can't do the work.

At the crisis, you know where you are in your own Universal Story. Know your part in the breakdown and you will see it in your story, too. Take back your power.

Excuse yourself from your writing and go for a walk. When you return, you will feel lighter and more carefree. You will know that you have taken back the authority over your story. Later, you freely admit to the obvious: that you easily fall victim and give up your power. Write down the emotions you were feeling. Give them to your character.

You know you have a distance to travel, but now conscious of how your emotions and beliefs negatively influence your writing and interfere with successfully completing your goal, you cannot go back to sleep. Step away from the story emotionally. Get your ego out of the way. View your story analytically. Rest assured that the difficulties that set out to destroy you at the crisis will ultimately propel you forward.

Only in time will you come to a place of true acceptance.

Writing is a marvel, miracle, and delight as words flow out of you from some unknown and sacred place. You suspect something else is involved as you read your own words. You often wonder who wrote such perfection. Stay vigilant. Do not fall victim to switching from reverence to assuming complete ownership and control over your creative process.

Crisis and the Show of Emotion

One of the most gratifying aspects of reading and going to the theater is the shared experience of living someone else's life. During a crisis, full expression demands that you get under the protagonist's skin and into her emotions.

PLOT WHISPER

Test the scene you have chosen for the crisis to learn if it fits the parameters.

On your plot planner the energy of your scenes rises in intensity after the second energetic marker of the recommitment scene. During this tumultuous period building up to the crisis, how many below-the-line scenes of introspection and planning by the protagonist occur? In all other scenes, does the energy of the story rise due to obstacles, antagonists, and insights into the character's issues (above-the-line scenes) and deepen what is introduced in the beginning? What does the protagonist still need to learn about herself, or more to the point, need to relearn and become conscious of in order to prevail at the end of the story?

To satisfy the Universal Story, this scene of highest intensity so far in the story generally hits around three-quarters into the entire page count. Does this apply to your plot's crisis? If not, are you satisfied with your reasons why?

Now, ask yourself how does the energy coalesce and explode at the crisis? Does the highest point in the story so far function primarily on an external dramatic action level?

What does the action in the crisis reveal about the character's internal makeup and emotional maturity?

Scan each scene in your story in order from the beginning and consider only the part(s) your protagonist plays in her own demise. Perhaps not all the scenes show her in her flawed state. Still, some scenes capture her not fully in her own power. What part of herself does she need to reclaim in order to be whole?

A story is about a character transforming her weaknesses into strengths.

Readers feel deep and intense emotions in their bodies and live moment by moment with the character. Stories tell us that we, too, can survive the dark night of the soul. We, too, can know the moment consciousness slays the ego.

At their core, stories are about character transformation. The crisis serves as a slap in the face, a wake-up call, the moment when the character becomes aware of life's deeper meaning. Life takes the protagonist by the shoulders and shakes her until she sees life and herself as both really are. The crisis jolts the character into a new acceptance, one in which transformation flourishes. Unless an event creates some sort of learning, awakening, or consciousness, it does not constitute a true crisis.

Think of the protagonist's crisis as the antagonist's climax where the antagonist(s) prevails and the protagonist fails. The protagonist is only as good as the antagonists.

Throughout the entire beginning and middle of a story, antagonists always are more powerful than the protagonist and seem always to find just the right buttons to push to bring out the worst in the protagonist. After the threshold following the crisis all that changes. For now . . . the antagonist(s) rule.

The height of the antagonist's power comes at the crisis when the protagonist is confronted by a moment of truth; thereafter, nothing is ever the same.

PLOT WHISPER

Ask youself, what part does the antagonist(s) play in the ultimate breakdown of the protagonist? View all the scenes that come before the crisis on your plot planner. Is there another antagonist who holds even greater power over the protagonist than the one at work at the crisis? If so, can that antagonist be integrated into the crisis? Perhaps the scene written now as the crisis actually holds only enough energy to qualify for placement in the scene sequence building to the crisis. This is the case with Lily's conversation with August in *The Secret Life of Bees*. Could a scene between the protagonist and some other antagonist build on that energy to create a true crisis, such as what happens when Lily goes on to battle herself in the honey room?

The Way Forward Is Destroyed

As we discussed earlier in this chapter, sometimes the crisis takes the form of two separate events written in two separate scenes. In this case, one scene hits the highest point so far in the story for the dramatic action plot and another scene moves even higher and affects the character emotional development plot separately. Or, the character emotional development crisis comes first and the dramatic action crisis follows. Generally, these two high points occur close together for maximum effect, though sometimes they occur separately and fall further apart.

In *Watership Down* by Richard Adams, the crisis for the character emotional plot hits at nearly the exact halfway point and also serves as the recommitment scene. Hazel leaves the new warren with one other rabbit, searching for female rabbits. This is a dangerous but important goal because without females, the new warren will die out when the last of the males dies.

However, because the reader knows Hazel sent Holly and a few others out in another direction for the same purpose, we come to realize that

Hazel's decision to go is reckless and filled with ego. The rabbits' survival is not dependent upon him going, and in doing so he jeopardizes the safety of all the other rabbits. Up to this point of the story, we have considered Hazel's actions heroic, acts of amazing bravery and courage. Now, as we read that he has been spotted by two men, one with a gun, and is shot down, the story builds to an unbearable pitch. Is our hero dead or holding on by a thread? We, the readers, and he, the hero, are forced to rethink his earlier behavior and the very definition of heroic acts of bravery.

This scene is followed by one dramatic action scene after another, until the dramatic action plot hits its highest point so far in the story. As a ruse, the recovered Hazel, healed and on another quest for does, sends Bigwig, his strongest ally, into a warren of evil rabbits. Bigwig accepts the mission, knowing the odds of success are small to none. Even so, the moment arrives when he must make a break from the evil warren with the females. At that very instant, the Chief Rabbit of the evil warren speaks up from behind him. This represents the crisis of maximum effect in the dramatic action plot. The Chief Rabbit holds all the power and controls the fates of Bigwig, Hazel, and the rest of the rabbits awaiting Bigwig's return with the female rabbits.

THE WRITER'S WAY

Feel free to push at the edges of the concepts offered in this book, to play with the unexpected, build excitement, and provide plot twists.

Stories are about characters resisting and struggling. You, as a writer, are at your best when you use the structure of the Universal Story to provide more energy and a more profound thematic significance even than the story on the page.

Learn the basics. Then, push aside everything you think you know and everything you like about the work of other writers. Go off in a totally new direction, your own unique direction.

Know about the energy of the Universal Story and you are better able to bypass a crisis yourself and everyday to write with a sense of consciousness. You are more concerned with the next sentence than reaching the end, more concerned with sending out queries than attaining an agent, more concerned with your next story than the reviews you receive.

The story comes through you. Your job is to present what comes in a pleasing form to the reader and audience. This takes setting yourself aside and means opening your mind to receive the greatest good of the story.

See your work as perfect no matter where in the process. Know that every day you sit down to write you improve your writing. Every time you look deeper into the structure of your story, you see an even more meaningful perfection awaiting you.

The relationship you have with your writing is reflective of your relationship with yourself.

CHARACTER EMOTIONAL DEVELOPMENT PROFILE FOR *WATERSHIP DOWN*

Protagonist's name: Hazel

Overall story goal: To find a new home

What stands in his way? Fear, predators, and the unknown

What does he stand to lose? His life

Flaws: Foolhardy

Strengths: Courageous, adventurous, knows how to work with others, speaks with simple honesty

Hate: Being shown up

Loves: Fiver

Fears: Predators

Dream: A safe new home

Figure 12. Character Emotional Development Profile for *Watership Down* by Richard Adams

CHAPTER TEN
TRANSFORMATION

I can be changed by what happens to me, but I refuse to be reduced by it.

—Maya Angelou

The crisis explodes with the greatest impact in the energetic flow of the story so far. The external action at the crisis destroys all routes back to the familiar ground upon which the protagonist previously stood. The crisis changes her and—this is extremely important—thus destroys all roads leading forward as well. The protagonist is now trapped; both the way back and the path forward are closed. The only choice open to her is to change who she is at her core. Only by doing this will she find her way.

Inner and Outer Change

All the outer events, ordeals, successes, and failures of the character constitute the dramatic action of a story and provide the catalyst for change. The transformation results from an inner crumbling that is manifest at the crisis, but it begins internally long before. This leaves the final quarter of the book for you to show the protagonist's ultimate regeneration from brokenness, fear, and alienation. Her rebirth is shown by the actions she takes to achieve her goal. Her changed behavior at the end of the story, compared to the way she acts at the beginning of the story, serves as proof that a transformation has occurred.

Each obstacle and antagonist in the dramatic action plot provides the protagonist with opportunities to learn about herself and thus advance her character emotional development plot. However, before she can transform, she first must become conscious of her strengths and weaknesses. As we've seen, the best antagonists act as mirrors for the protagonist to see who she is and how she sabotages herself.

In the middle of the story, the protagonist may begin to suspect the part she plays in her failures and problems, but until the crisis she doesn't understand completely the source of those problems. Above all, she hasn't faced up to *herself*. When confronted with problems, she points to the faults and flaws of others and blames them, while denying and ignoring her own faults and flaws.

The crisis strips her of all her defenses and excuses. It ties the protagonist's character emotional development plot thematically to the rest of the story. She no longer can hide her head in the sand, talk her way out of problems, rationalize her failings, or blame others for her inadequacies. She is forced to look deeply at herself and, because of what happens at the crisis, finally see the part she plays in her own failure. She must acknowledge that she is the root of her own problems. The crisis awakens her to full consciousness and begins the process toward acceptance and ultimate wisdom.

Some people believe that we come into the world to heal a specific wound, but that, at birth, we forget our task. Most of us spend our lives unconscious of this deeper destiny.

The opposite is true in a story. What happens throughout the story makes it *impossible* for the protagonist to remain unconscious. The crisis in the middle shakes her awake. Only when conscious can she face the greatest challenge of the entire story—the climax at the end—and survive and triumph.

In Chapter Five, we examined the structure of the screenplay *Juno*. Those same goals that were part of the emotional development plot directly influence the climax of the story.

From the beginning of the story, Juno's external, dramatic action struggle is to decide what to do about being pregnant. The unresolved emotion from her backstory loss, when her mother abandoned her as a child, has lodged itself in Juno and is interfering with her success in finding a family for her baby. She knows intellectually that the wife of the couple she has chosen is committed and desperate to be a mother; she also knows that the husband wants a divorce. To choose the woman without the man means Juno must emotionally accept what she, because of her backstory, believes is an imperfect arrangement. In order to find a way out of this dilemma, Juno revises her belief system. In so doing, she releases her negative emotions and frees herself from the power her backstory wound held over her.

The Threshold after the Crisis

After the crisis, the energy of the Universal Story ebbs again. In Chapter Eight, we discussed the importance of the threshold at the end of the beginning of a story. This threshold determines whether the protagonist enters the heart of the story world in the middle of the book willingly or reluctantly. The threshold the protagonist is about to cross, the one at the end of the middle, determines what self-knowledge and rediscovered skills she takes with her into the final quarter of the overall story.

However, before crossing the threshold, the character and the reader need time to take things in, adjust, plan, and come to terms. Reeling after her experiences in the crisis, the protagonist retreats, stripped of who she has been and with a sense that everyone and everything has abandoned her. The aftermath of the crisis is a time of reflection to give the protagonist and the audience an opportunity to catch their collective breath. Here, the protagonist feels a change of heart and mind as she searches for meaning in what just happened.

The dramatic action at the crisis causes the protagonist to open her eyes, perhaps for the first time. She sees that external events are not responsible for keeping her from achieving her goals. It's her own choices that create the problem.

The time the protagonist spends after the crisis and before ascending to the climax at the book's end indicates to readers and audiences the effect of the crisis on the character. However, not until the protagonist acts in response to the most intense event of the entire story at the climax will the reader know the full extent of the protagonist's maturation and to what depth she has truly transformed.

The crisis in the Pulitzer Prize–winning novella, *The Old Man and the Sea* by Ernest Hemingway, is not a crisis in the usual sense. Instead, it is a change and increase in energetic intensity.

Three-quarters of the way into the story, Santiago successfully kills a marlin that is larger than any he has seen in all his years of fishing. The battle is intense, sends him to his knees, and nearly kills him. But still he ends up with that which he most desires. This feels like the antithesis of what a crisis usually represents. Still, on a purely energetic level, this action serves as the highest point in the entire story so far. In the pages that follow, the energy drops in preparation for the climax as Santiago lashes the giant fish to his skiff, savoring his success.

Cause and Effect

Events in real life often seem to occur randomly and make no sense. The Universal Story is satisfying because it gives these events structure and suggests causes for them. When we read stories in which causes are clearly traceable to effects we gain insight into how to control life by the responses we make. In other words, the Universal Story gives us hope for handling our personal lives.

To dig for the cause of the situation in which she now finds herself, the protagonist must begin to understand what choices brought her here. This will offer clues about what to do next.

In a purely action-driven story, the protagonist's analysis is at the dramatic action level, as she looks only at external events and their consequences. In a character-driven story, the protagonist takes into account her own personal character emotional development at each step along the way. As I hope you realize by this point, a combination of these two styles of writing—action-driven and character-driven; right-brained and left-brained—works best.

The protagonist reacts emotionally as she processes the events. Readers and audiences are better able to identify and connect to the protagonist when she shows the full range of emotional effects the crisis has on her.

In Chapter Three, we discussed how cause and effect within scenes allows you to seamlessly lead the reader to each major turning point by linking the cause in one scene to the effect in the next scene. This sequencing allows the energy of the story to rise smoothly. If the sequence breaks down, scenes come out of the blue, and your story turns episodic. The reader becomes disconcerted.

In Chapter Five, I talked about how to use cause and effect to convey emotion in the protagonist. In scene one, a character emotionally responds to an event. In scene two, we see the outcome of that emotional response, which, in turn, becomes cause for another effect. Each scene is organic; seeds planted in the first scene create the effect in the next.

Now, at the crisis, we use the same cause-and-effect structure to help the protagonist make sense of how she got into the mess she is in.

Connecting the Dots

This is a time when the character decides, because of what happened at the crisis, whether she takes on the mantle of the victim or that of the victor and thus, determines the final quarter of the story. The reader, of course, knows the protagonist is no victim and enthusiastically reads on to learn when she discovers that for herself.

First, the protagonist requires time to take apart what just happened before she can put herself back together again. In other words, she needs space to rest, re-evaluate, and revise before forging ahead. This space after the crisis affords her the time to see what is at work and parts the veil, so she can glimpse at the essence of herself and life around her. Before she can rise up in her true power at the last quarter of the book, she must understand what she stands for now.

At its core, this time of regrouping takes place on a purely cognitive level. Though the protagonist may assemble the resources she plans to take forward with her, until she takes her first step toward her final goal she remains in the middle of the story and, as yet, has not entered the final one-quarter of the story.

PLOT WHISPER

Use a felt-tip pen to link the scenes from the beginning of your story all the way to the crisis. However, you can only draw a line from one scene to the next if the dramatic action in one scene causes what happens in the next.

Ask yourself at each scene, does what happens in this scene cause the character to do what she does in the next scene? If the answer is yes, then draw a line connecting the two scenes. If the answer is no, leave the scenes separated.

The drop in energy allows for the reader and audience to rebuild anticipation and expectation for what will happen when the protagonist ultimately leaves the middle of the story and sets out for the climax at the end of the story.

As the protagonist considers the thoughts that have held her captive, she can mourn what was. But rather than hold onto those same old beliefs and continue to retard her progress, now she is free to reshape her life by speaking and acting in her own truth. Once she develops a new belief system, a shift occurs in her life. Having wakened to her potential, she is finally clear to seize that which she most longs for.

The drop in the energy of a Universal Story is symbolized on the plot planner by a downward line after the crisis. This entire downward line can be viewed as the threshold separating the middle of the story from the end. Literally, a threshold is a doorsill or the starting point of an experience. On the plot planner and in the Universal Story, this threshold encompasses the integration of and preparatory time needed after the crisis and before the actual crossing over into the final quarter of the story. The length of the line as the energy contracts depends on your story. In high-action stories, the drop in intensity may occur over one short scene.

In the screenplay for the thriller *Salt* by Kurt Wimmer, for instance, after the crisis, Salt, taken into custody as a traitor, begins her slow walk up the staircase, chained and defeated. A moment later she explodes, kicking ass. Now, because of what she sufferd at the crisis, she knows who the true villain is.

In a quieter, more internal character-driven story, the threshold may last for scenes and even for several chapters.

The young adult trilogy *The Hunger Games* by Suzanne Collins is set in the future in a place known as North America (only tangentially related to the North America we're familiar with). The end of the beginning scene of the story shows sixteen-year-old Katniss Everdeen step forward to take her sister's place in the Games, knowing she is volunteering to fight to the death on live television.

In the middle of the story Katniss nearly starves, is nearly blown up, burned by a wall of fire, and attacked by jabberjays. But not until she faces her partner, does Katniss suffer the true crisis. Peeta is cut and bleeding and near death. Only Katniss can save him.

She stops the damage from spreading, then half-carries and half-guides Peeta to a cave where he can recover.

The cave serves metaphorically as the threshold, and as the painfully horrific dramatic action slows to a stop, the reader breathes a sigh of relief. Tension from the looming reality of the Games and her opponents continues, which makes this time of resting and regrouping poignant and, at the same time, because of what awaits them, tragic, too. Katniss and the reader know the worst is yet to come.

This brief rest before the final crescendo gives Katniss a chance to deepen her understanding of not only herself and her partner but the rules of the game, as well. The next scenes are devoted to Katniss's nursing of Peeta, leaving only to hunt for food. During this much-welcomed break in the action, the reader learns more about Katniss's backstory. Then, Katniss uses what she learns about herself and Peeta and the game to enact her next move, and the ending begins.

PLOT WHISPER

Make a list of the attributes and knowledge the protagonist does not have at the beginning or middle of the story and must acquire, relearn, or rediscover in order to prevail at the end of your story.

Refer to that list as you analyze scene by scene the middle section of the plot planner. Indicate on sticky notes where the protagonist's self-sabotaging behavior reveals itself. Affix the notes to the plot planner above the corresponding scenes.

Determine how the character's weak spots contribute to the crisis. Add those notes toward the end of the middle of the story. Next, make notes on the downward line of the plot planner about:

- Where is best for the threshold to take place
- How long the threshold lasts
- What the protagonist learns while at the threshold

Crossing the Threshold Again

No matter how safe she may feel, the protagonist soon learns that every form of refuge has its price. The longer she dawdles at the threshold, the greater the price she will be forced to pay by having to replay the same mistakes over and over again. No matter how much she beats herself up and loathes herself for the disaster that has ensued, she must step forward into the end of the story.

One conscious outward movement symbolizes the closing of one door and the opening of another. In that step forward, the protagonist's life expands.

In plotting your story, the moment when your protagonist crosses over the threshold into the end deserves emphasis. Show the character's emotional anticipation of the moment of crossing, the emotional and physical sensations as it happens, and her reaction when the action is complete and the character understands she has entered the true belly of the beast.

The crisis kills the character's ego in return for wisdom. The death of the old character gives birth to a new one. Old tensions released during the crisis allow new energy to grow in the protagonist.

In *The Hunger Games*, while Katniss and Peeta rest in the cave, healing themselves and learning more about each other, the reader learns more about the protagonist and her backstory, and about the boy she always thought was her enemy, who also satisfies the romantic plot, though there is a boy back home who could ultimately interfere with a successful resolution of this plot. Together, Katniss and Peeta hear the Gamemakers' announcement offering them what they need to survive, but at the price of having to leave the relative safety of the cave. Katniss knows the help being offered is a ruse to get her to move. The lull in the action has gone on for too long. Her acceptance that the viewing audience back home clamors for excitement shows that she has integrated what she has learned during her time spent in the threshold between the crisis and the end of the story.

Peeta, still too weak to be moved, refuses to let Katniss risk her life for him. Falsely, she agrees, but he catches her in the lie and threatens to go, too. What is she supposed to do? she asks him.

"'Sit here and watch you die?' I say. He must know that's not an option."

But even as she says that, she is still playing the hunger games, a game that continues on to the death of all your opponents. The last person standing wins. She knows the audience watching the games would hate her if she let him die.

"And frankly, I would hate myself, too, if I didn't even try."

"I won't die. I promise. If you promise not to go," he says.

Katniss, now wise to the way the game is played, tricks Peeta. The moment she feeds him sugar berries she collects and laces with sleep syrup, she crosses into the final quarter of the entire story.

Overcoming the Guardians at the Threshold

The threshold is guarded by forces that will prevent anyone who is not ready, not fit for the final leg of the journey, from passing on. They test the protagonist and try to lure her away from what she most desires. They caution her to reconsider before stepping over into the great unknown.

Threshold guardians often appear giant and frightening. They can be lions, dragons, serpents, winged bulls, dogs, and beasts. Or, they can be forces within the protagonist, forces that are non-sentient but are worse than any ogre, halting her at the point of transformation. In either case, they make explicit the demand that the protagonist set aside her old personality if she wishes to cross to the next realm.

Well aware now, she knows she can no longer afford to be halted by any of these forces:

- Fear
- Suffering
- A perceived state of lack and insufficiency
- Grasping
- Clinging
- Compulsive negative thinking
- Addictive behavior
- Pain of past hurts
- Fear of future unknowns
- Victim-consciousness
- Blaming
- Guilt

At the threshold, for one heartbeat she is suspended, straddling both worlds and present in neither. When she crosses, having abandoned old emotional ideas that no longer serve her, the horizon enlarges and intensifies. The dramatic action at the crisis forces the protagonist to see both physically and intuitively the bigger picture of her life and the world around her.

Revealing the Backstory

If you have been able to hold back and have not revealed the backstory thus far, now as the character stands on the verge of change, is an acceptable time. The event that rocked her in the past often sheds light on why she has acted as she has. It shows where the beliefs, fears, and prejudices come from that have tripped her up for so long. Often, what she finds is that the negative thoughts she carries belong to someone else.

CNN reporter Anderson Cooper comments that his father's death when Anderson was just a young lad caused him to believe he was not the man he had been born to be. If I may be so bold, I wonder if, in fact, perhaps his destiny was to become *exactly* the man he has become. His father's death, though tragic and sad, ultimately afforded him the strength and purpose to walk fully into his power.

In the first couple of lines of *The Lace Reader* by Brunonia Barry, the protagonist gives herself two names (foreshadowing the end of the story) and proclaims her flaw by reporting that she lies "all the time." These first lines set up the major thrust of the story, which is for the reader to solve the mystery of who she truly is. Because the mystery is locked in the protagonist's backstory, the author weaves flashbacks and memories into the fabric of the front story.

The crisis for the front story takes place near the second energetic marker at the halfway point when the villain physically grabs the protagonist. By now, because of the protagonist's propensity for lying, the reader is desperate to learn who the protagonist truly is.

In the threshold after the front story crisis, the protagonist's sense of responsibility to the woman who has been portrayed as her great-aunt serves as a threshold guardian by preventing her from moving toward her goal of escaping the ghosts and demons of her past. A realtor interested in selling the recently inherited house and oblivious to the protagonist's pain pushes her forward. The male character who represents the romance plot slows her escape by inviting her out on a date. In the pull to stay as she is and the push to evolve, cracks begin appearing in her lies. The longer she stays in her childhood setting, the worse she suffers and the more of her backstory we learn.

The crisis of the backstory is revealed at the customary crisis location around three-quarters of the way into the story when the protagonist attempts suicide. The threshold after the backstory crisis ties back to the earlier threshold established after the front story crisis. It is only now, during the threshold, that concrete clues show her flaw of lying is directed inward. Yes, she has been lying to other characters and to the reader, too, but now slowly, the reader begins to understand that the protagonist ultimately has been lying mostly to herself.

The woman we are told is the protagonist's mother acts as a threshold guardian when she attempts to hide the protagonist on an island, believing she is not ready, not fit for the final leg of her journey. And, it's true, the protagonist is not ready. The scenes she spends being hospitalized and looked after by the love interest belong on the downward line of the plot planner directly after the crisis. Only after she rediscovers her inner strength enough to defy all of the threshold guardians does she step into the end of the story and the plot planner line begins to ascend.

RE-EXAMINING THE PROTAGONIST'S GOALS AND PURPOSES

While in the downward energy of the threshold, the protagonist has the ability to see and choose between two realities. One is a past filled with whining and complaining, old habits and desires, trapped in fear and anger, self-pity, guilt, blame, and all other avoidance strategies, such as being attached to memories and thinking and talking about the past.

The other reality is made up of new values, structures, and choices. No longer controlled by desires, external forces, and instincts of the past, the protagonist surveys resources, finances, values, emotional desires, possessions, addictions, and relationships. She works with intuition until she has gained a perspective above, below, and on all sides of her life.

THE WRITER'S WAY

When we get hit with a crisis in real life, we accept either what is and move on in a transformed way or we return to unconsciousness and live crippled and victimized.

One reason people seem to go back to sleep, acting in ways that indicate oblivion to the deeper meaning of any trauma, is because they lack knowledge about the value of time spent in the threshold. Without assessing what went wrong and taking responsibility, we often repeat our mistakes.

On the left side of your journal, list the strengths and allies you brought with you into your writing life when you began and the ones you have acquired since. Note any wisdom you have gained about yourself, about plot and the Universal Story, and about your story.

On the opposite page, list the behaviors, belief patterns, and antagonists you are ready to release before crossing into the final stretch of completing your story.

Now cross out the behaviors and belief patterns that no longer serve you.

Circle the strengths that will help you achieve your goal of finishing your story and those qualities you plan to take forward with you.

This time of assessment gives her insight as she reorients herself from the material, external world of the ego to a more internal, compassionate focus. Now she may become aware of the influence her backstory has had on her current status. She understands how the crisis or pain in her backstory created core beliefs about life itself, beliefs she now understands are flawed and without value in light of all she has been through. She understands that no matter what experiences she has had in the world to convince her otherwise, she is a light at the center of the universe. The reader senses an alert stillness within the character. Along with renewed enthusiasm comes a new wave of creative energy.

The protagonist has three choices: stay locked in this moment forever (and therefore, frustrated), attempt to go back (which, as the reader already knows, is impossible because all ways back have been destroyed), or change. Action arising out of insight is more effective than action arising out of negativity. Any action is better than no action. She *must* move forward. With a new sense of responsibility to herself, the protagonist finds value as she builds new attitudes and sensibilities and plans a new life for herself.

Often during this deliberation, the protagonist is offered the goal she has been lusting for and which represents her old personality, only to realize she does not want it any longer. Now, she has to redefine what she does want.

Unlike in real life, in stories the protagonist—by definition the character most changed by the dramatic action—cannot fall back into unconsciousness. She must take action. The author decides whether the character moves from the crisis into acceptance only or whether she pursues a new goal for herself with enthusiasm. A clearly defined goal helps refocus the reader for the final quarter of the story.

The threshold following the crisis is a time for the main character to reinvent herself. She asks what she will take with her as she enters the future. What attitudes, habits, and relationships will she keep and which will she leave behind? She recreates and reorganizes her self-identity.

Crises that have love-related issues at their core—divorce, the death of a loved one, emotional abuse, abandonment, betrayal, adultery—always demand the healing of emotional issues. Days or years of repressed data flood into the protagonist's consciousness as she enters her own heart and searches for lessons to be learned. Leaving behind all familiar thought patterns, she searches for her own truth.

In the novel *The Bridges of Madison County* by Robert James Waller, Francesca Johnson, the protagonist of the story, suffers a crisis when she falls in love with a traveling photographer while her husband and children are away. A series of flashbacks allows the energy to drop and the reader to connect the dots before she steps into the final quarter of the story and takes the first steps toward severing herself from the relationship.

In the safety of the threshold, the protagonist owns up to her errors, flaws, and negative behaviors that block her success. She understands how her attitudes blind her to the truth about herself and the people and the world around her. She accepts her shadow side and develops a broader sense of responsibility for healing herself. In so doing, she hopes, either consciously or unconsciously, that perhaps, by healing herself, she helps heal the world.

THE EFFECT OF THE CRISIS

The effect of the crisis on the character in a character-driven, spiritual journey changes the character. The crisis becomes her moment of great awakening and allows the protagonist to make decisions that change her life entirely.

Now that her life is most out of control, she becomes receptive to guidance she would not have welcomed earlier. Perhaps for the first time, she becomes aware of disturbing emotions and impulses within her and what they lead her to do. She understands what creates stress for her and what motivates her best performance. She identifies nonverbal clues in how others feel and begins to develop empathy. She considers new ways to listen, talk, and act that resolve conflicts instead of escalating them and develops strategies to negotiate for win-win solutions.

Consciously aware, she takes in all the sensory details around her. She knows from earlier scenes not to think her troubles have ended. Of all the previous challenges, nothing compares to the one that now beckons at the end of the book. She fully expects her pain to grow worse before it gets better.

Stretch the space of this critical time between the crisis and the time she steps into the end of the story in a scene in order to further the suspense of the story. Suspense engages the reader. Every threshold between one symbolic place and another has the potential to alert the reader and audience that the character is transitioning into the unknown. Thresholds create excitement, expectancy, and an element of fear of the unknown in both the character and the reader.

The protagonist willingly, honestly, and accurately names her own culpability. Confronted with a potentially life-threatening and ego-threatening situation, she sees herself for who she is, flaws and strengths alike. She believes she is going to live a better life from now on and makes plans for all she intends to do.

Thresholds Hold Tension

By slowing the action and drama after the crisis, when the energy rises to announce the final quarter, the story moves quickly and with maximum impact to the end.

Whether the threshold to the next step is open and invites discovery or is closed, thresholds signify a space of perfect balance. Something has happened and something will happen. Only this exact moment is real. A threshold is a point of truth.

The protagonist estimates what is necessary for ultimate success in achieving her goal. She gathers the attributes, things, and people to take forward with her on the final journey to the end. She leaves behind everything that does not serve the highest good.

CHAPTER ELEVEN
THE CLIMAX

A man is but the product of his thoughts. What he thinks, he becomes.

—Mohandas Gandhi

The final quarter of the story shows the protagonist taking action without hesitation. The character may have thought about the actions she intends to take to accomplish her goal and even voiced them, but until she acts her words are meaningless. The moment she moves toward her long-term goal, the final one-quarter of the story begins. The dramatic action is designed to get the protagonist to the right place at the right time to seize back her personal power from the antagonist that best represents the thematic significance of the entire story. In *The Lace Reader*, Calvin represents all that the protagonist has lost. To break free of the hell in which her fear has held her for fifteen years, she must face him, face her greatest fear.

At the end of the story, every moment now breathes anticipation of the crowning glory of the entire story: the climax.

In *The Hunger Games*, Katniss leaves the safety of the cave after drugging Peeta, and heads out alone to potential disaster in the final quarter of the story. The night is bitterly cold "as if the Gamesmakers have sent an infusion of frozen air across the arena." She finds the correct location and seizes what she needs to keep Peeta alive, suffers from a knife slice across her forehead, and gets pinned to the ground by one of her fiercest opponents. The skills she learned earlier in the game from an opponent-turned-ally save her. She makes it back to the cave and

189

Peeta. When she departs the cave this time, she leaves with Peeta who is still weak from his wounds. The story has a sense of finality about it. The Games are nearly done. She goes on to gather information, fight mutations, listen to a boy die, and watch Peeta weaken more.

To cap it off, the moment she believes she and Peeta have won, the Gameskeepers announce another change in the rules: "Only one winner may be allowed."

She knows she can't let Peeta kill himself in order to let her win "because if he dies, I'll never go home, not really. I'll spend the rest of my life in this arena trying to think my way out." She's learned what it will cost her spirit to win at Peeta's expense. Instead, she fulfills her destiny: She stands up against the corruption of the Capital and the Gameskeepers when she opens "the pouch and pour[s] a few spoonfuls of [poison] into his palm. Then I fill my own." This act of defiance signifies that Katniss is willing to die rather than sacrifice her very soul.

Finally she understands that the Gamemakers' plan "will only work if I play along with them." With a broader view and deeper understanding of the world at large, she shrugs off the victim's cloak. She holds the power over her own life because only she can give them what they want and only she can take it away: instead of one winner, two deaths.

The final quarter of your story represents the end of the Universal Story and is comprised of three parts:

1. The buildup to the climax
2. The climax itself
3. The resolution

The Buildup to the Climax

The buildup to the climax is a sequence of scenes that sets up the crowning glory of the entire story. In these scenes, the protagonist reclaims the power she relinquished to other people, places, and things. She responds to external conflict with actions and behaviors that show her breaking free from the patterns she has exhibited in the past. She takes action that shows she is moving toward who she was born to be.

Empowered by the knowledge gained at the crisis, she now understands the rules of the life she has chosen to enter. She is wiser and more powerful than she has been anywhere else in the story. The antagonists, though, have grown in ferocity, too. The challenges intensify.

Conflict continues to drive the plot. Obstacles fuel the conflict as the character struggles to reach her goal. As the protagonist nears her goal, the obstacles take on greater and greater levels of difficulty.

During this final sequence, the protagonist may feel as if she has transcended the physical and material world. And transcendence always leads to triumph. The protagonist knows from the experience at the crisis, however, not to be ruled by her ego or become overly confident. She struggles to hold her balance and move forward step-by-step toward the final prize. She is no longer interested in strengthening herself by diminishing others. With increased awareness and new consciousness, and with the ego no longer running her life, she steps fully into her power.

For example, *One for the Money*, a mystery novel by Janet Evanovich, tells the story of Stephanie who is desperate for money, self-possessed, and sure of herself. An old flame, now a bail jumper, foils her attempts to turn him in so she can collect the money and pay off her back rent. The old flame interferes with her goal and thus serves as an antagonist, as do her circumstances. But the main antagonist is a villain determined to stop Stephanie by any means available, including murder.

At the crisis, Stephanie pulls back the curtain in her bedroom. A woman is cut and beaten and tied at an odd angle to her fire escape. She is barely alive. The villain calls. He whispers promises of a fate even worse for Stephanie. In that moment, Stephanie's assured and arrogant self dies.

Twenty-eight pages later, she crosses the threshold into the end of the story, as evidenced when she takes action toward her revised goal of finding the villain. Empowered and self-assertive, she is both excited and unnerved as she makes changes in her life. The reader knows she has begun the transformation and ascent to the climax. We can see elements of this transformation when, rather than barging into an office looking for information as she had done earlier, Stephanie waits patiently to be announced.

The outcomes in her life improve internally and externally. She discovers a sense of self-sufficiency. In time, she changes from a psychologically immature and emotionally scarred woman to a courageous, self-responsible, and assured individual.

From the moment the protagonist marches into the final quarter of the story, the action in each scene is active and dramatic and soars above the plot planner line. Gone are any openings for flashbacks, backstory, or explanation to slow down the action. We don't need internal monologue or author intrusion. Now, the momentum builds swiftly.

This is no time for passivity. Nor is it a time for overly aggressive and controlling action. The end is a time for innovation and creativity, a time for facing all the external forces of evil. The protagonist sees the world around her through the wisdom she has gained because of the crisis. Now she understands the gift she's been given.

For her, the world is now the same and yet completely different. She realizes that events are not random and arbitrary. Instead they are connected, there to challenge her so she can become strong in anticipation of the climax. Those she viewed through the prism of her old consciousness as antagonists, she now appreciates as teachers.

No longer isolated, she more freely expresses her feelings and willingly asks others for help. Each time she acts with her rediscovered self-knowledge and skills, and successfully resolves both the internal and the external conflicts she confronts, she is rewarded with benefits, often unexpected. Each time she speaks up, she gathers courage and prepares herself for the final confrontation at the climax.

The Climax Itself

The climax is the point of highest drama in your story, the crowning moment when the thematic significance of your story becomes clear to the reader. Just as it looks as if all is permanently lost for the protagonist, at the climax she delivers the gift.

At the climax, all the major forces come together for a final clash. Your protagonist demonstrates her new awareness, skill, strength, belief, and/or personal power. At the climax, as her new self, she now is able to confront antagonists and conquer challenges that her old self could not.

The fourth energetic marker and the climax itself show the character fully united with her new or rediscovered self-knowledge and skills, understanding of the world, and sense of responsibility through her actions and her words. In the end, the protagonist confronts and overcomes a final foe.

Throughout *East of Eden*, Cal's battle has been purely internal. Within him has raged the archetypal war between good and evil. Steinbeck adapts the biblical names of Cain and Abel, driving home the thematic significance of the battle by making Aron blond and Cal dark. Aron is innocent, all good. Cal has a dark and secret side.

The book begins before the protagonist is even born, so Cal's backstory wound unfolds gradually throughout the book. When he is eleven, he manipulates Aron for the first time. After that, he surrenders his will to the belief he is evil.

By the time Cal arrives at the climax, he has begun to understand that the choices one makes, not one's blood, determine destiny. To fully reclaim his power, Cal openly confesses to his father the litany of evils Cal has perpetuated against his brother and his father, all of which he has relentlessly been punishing himself for. This sincere and loving confession of Cal's is action he could never have undertaken earlier in the story. He first needed to suffer and learn. When he no longer defines himself by the evil of his mother's sins but rather by his choices, he embodies the thematic significance of the story. Cal reclaims his own individual power and proves by his actions who he truly is. Because of his rediscovered skills of compassion, Cal gains what he has always wanted: his father's love. With the housekeeper and family mentor's help, Cal's father forgives him, thus freeing Cal to forgive himself and become the head of the family.

Another character may accompany the protagonist to the final confrontation, but the spotlight shines only on the main character. Ultimately she and she alone faces her greatest fear, does the final deed, and accomplishes that which she always intended to do.

PLOT WHISPER

Ask yourself, which scene most dramatically shows your protagonist demonstrating her transformed self?

When you know the answer to that question, you have your climax. The climax, in turn, informs all the other scenes in the entire project.

Now, add sticky notes for all the scenes in the final quarter of your story up to and including the climax. Determine the protagonist's greatest foe. Design the dramatic action around getting the protagonist to a final confrontation with the antagonist.

Indicate on the correct color sticky note the character emotional development she undergoes in each scene as she nears the climax. Include one sticky note for the climax, too.

Put up sticky notes for scenes where thematically significant elements exist.

It is best if the dramatic action plot, the character emotional development plot, and the thematic significance all collide at the same moment. But even if they occur in different scenes, the three plot lines must show the final confrontation of the greatest challenge and the resolution of the major conflict.

The climax does not have to be full of explosions and death. What this most important scene *does* have to have is *meaning to the overall story*.

The actions required of the protagonist at the climax would have been too much for her anywhere else in the story. She first needed to go through the experiences described in the story in order to prevail at the climax. Now, the moment is all hers. Beginnings hook readers. Endings create fans.

Tying the Dramatic Action to the Thematic Significance Plot in the Climax

A simple introduction to what makes up the protagonist's emotional development in the beginning of the story deepens at the first energetic marker as a shift or reversal outside of the character sends her into the heart of the story world. The protagonist introduced in the beginning quarter of a story spends twice that time in the cauldron of dramatic action in the middle. In both the beginning one-quarter of the story and into the middle of the story, the character's emotional makeup is revealed through successively challenging events that are linked by cause and effect.

At the climax, the newly created self confronts her greatest foe and prevails in a way she never could have at the beginning of the story. The healing of this schism shows itself at the climax.

PLOT WHISPER

Stand back from your plot planner. Analyze the scene notes affixed to the final quarter of your plot planner.

Do the scenes build in intensity from the first scene of the end to the climax?

If not, why not? Search for ways to escalate the tension in scenes nearest the climax.

Does each scene lead the reader to form a belief about how the story should end? Surprise the reader instead and deliver a twist.

What is the energetic intensity of the climax in your story? Increase the conflict, tension, and suspense.

Of all the characters in Fitzgerald's *The Great Gatsby*, Nick, who serves as the narrator, is the only character in the story changed by the dramatic action, thus making him also the protagonist. (To remind you, the definition of the protagonist is the character most changed by the dramatic action in the story. If there are other characters who are changed by the dramatic action in your story, then the protagonist is determined as the one who is most changed.)

THE WRITER'S WAY

For you as a writer, the crowning glory comes each time you complete a story all the way through to the end. You find yourself changed, wiser, calmer, and clearer about what a writer's life truly entails. Even so, you may find yourself flummoxed when it comes to creating just the right climax for your story.

One solution is to approach the problem through the theme. For instance, one writer I know constructed a story that revolved around the relationship between a protagonist and her father, representing the universal archetype of father and daughter. In her own life, the writer had unresolved issues with her father. Still, she was determined to write with truth and emotion the end of a story about a daughter reconciled with her father.

The first time she wrote the climax, it bogged down in self-pity. The story ended angry and unresolved.

She wrote another climax, this time afraid of expressing her own pent-up feelings. The story ended superficial and clichéd.

The writer understood that in order for her to accept new ideas, her old personality must die. Only then could she embrace all possibilities for the outcome to her protagonist and ultimately discover the unexpected.

Some may point to Gatsby as the protagonist. What counts with thematic significance is not even a dramatic change, such as the transformation from alive to dead in Gatsby's case. Rather it is how the dramatic action creates a long-term emotional change or transformation in the character.

Nick sets his own thematic significance in the book in Chapter Three when he states that he is one of the few honest people he has known. Because he is the narrator, the reader is curious to know if he is reliable or not. Does Nick have a clear sense of himself from his time in the war? Or, does he need to learn more about himself before he can accurately judge himself and others? By the end of the story, Nick understands that he has only begun to live up to his initial assessment of himself.

We could make a thematic significance statement that encompasses the emotional transformation Nick undergoes from the beginning and throughout to the end of the story: Only with maturity and assuming personal and moral responsibility are we able to accurately judge ourselves and others.

The Great Gatsby, as with all classic stories, deals in universal themes. Along with Nick's personal thematic significance, there is also an overall meaning or thematic significance for the entire story: Ambition for money and another's man's wife leads to self-destruction. The dramatic action in the scene at the climax of the book proves this theme.

Thematic Elements at the End

In making choices about what to include and not to include when you write a climax you need to focus on details: how that moment feels, tastes, and smells. How does the protagonist look at her moment of triumph, and what does she do? Specific is always better than general.

The thematic significance or deeper meaning of a story dictates the final layer in the selection, organization, nuances, and details of the story.

The dramatic meaning of your piece comes from scenes that are played out moment-by-moment on the page through action and dialogue. The emotional meaning always comes from the characters. The thematic meaning ties your entire story together. It's the reason you write your story, what you hope to prove, what the story is about. Theme is beneath the apparent subject or surface of the story; it is the deeper subject you are exploring.

Of course, there is always a lot more going on in a story than just the one- or two-sentence description of the theme, but a thematic significance statement attempts to represent the primary essence of your story.

For instance, the primary essence of Ursula Hegi's novel *Stones from the River* is the universality of being different. The protagonist of the story is a dwarf and represents anyone who has ever felt undesirable or different and tried to fit in. Eventually she learns that being different is a secret that we all share.

What do you keep coming back to in your writing?

F. Scott Fitzgerald continually fought to achieve material success and ultimately lost. Partly because of this, he was preoccupied with and fascinated by wealth and the lives of the wealthy. At the same time he envied the life of the privileged classes, he also saw its emptiness and came to believe that the adoption of materialism by the American public ultimately corrupted our idealism. Thus, his own personal themes directly influenced the theme of *The Great Gatsby*. Though a story about characters set in the United States in the 1920s, *The Great Gatsby* embodies the Universal Story about a man who, having clawed his way from rags to riches, finds wealth does not bring him happiness.

Like Fitzgerald, you start writing your story with a passion or, at the least, an interest in getting to the bottom of something. You have a reason for writing the story, though you may not be completely clear about what that reason is. Define it and you have found your theme. Explore the themes of your own life and you likely will stumble upon a theme or two of your story.

When you have grasped the thematic significance of your story, work your way through the scenes from the climax back to the beginning. Looking at the beginning quarter of the story compared to the climax, ask yourself where you began introducing the theme.

Read through the beginning quarter of the story and underline all the details you use in a scene. Switch them up to reflect the thematic significance.

For instance, in the first chapter of *The Great Gatsby*, Fitzgerald, keeping in mind his theme ambition for money and another's man's wife leads to self-destruction, shows different types of wealth: for example the difference between people who inherit money versus those who have only recently acquired their wealth. He also explores what defines self, and he points out different sorts of physical, mental, and emotional destruction.

Fitzgerald uses the most obvious and direct methods for building thematic significance through the advancement of the other two plotlines themselves—dramatic action and character emotional development—and through dialogue and narrative.

For instance, dialogue in Chapter One reveals a piece of the theme and, at the same time, part of Daisy's character emotional development. Early in the chapter, Nick, the narrator, learns that Daisy's husband is having an affair. In a conversation between Nick and Daisy about Daisy's young daughter, Nick understands she knows about the affair, too, when she says:

> "Well, she [her daughter] was less than an hour old and Tom was God knows where. I woke up out of the ether with an utterly abandoned feeling and asked the nurse right away if it was a boy or a girl. She told me it was a girl, and so I turned my head away and wept. 'All right,' I said. 'I'm glad it's a girl. And I hope she'll be a fool—that's the best thing a girl can be in this world, a beautiful little fool.' "

This belief of Daisy's creates morbid curiosity and urges the reader to keep reading. Thematically, her dialogue shows how Daisy's life of wealth is destroying her sense of herself and that of her baby girl.

Other techniques of deepening thematic significance may be sufficiently subtle that they do not even penetrate the reader's consciousness. Nevertheless, the use of mood, setting, and metaphor carry as much power as the other more obvious clues.

Fitzgerald describes Daisy's house as a Georgian Colonial mansion. The image evokes established wealth. He emphasizes Daisy's purity through the use of the color white. For a whisper of destruction, he adds red, the color of fire. These sorts of details are not random accidents. They are carefully planned out to convey the deepest thematic significance.

To write a lasting and meaningful story, don the hat of a sleuth. In each rewrite, search for all the ways to deepen the thematic significance of your stories. Your readers may never uncover the deliberate care that went into the formation of every detail of your story. They will be left to ponder the meaning you set forth, possibly even be changed by your story's theme.

In *To Kill a Mockingbird*, Harper Lee introduces Scout as a hotheaded, outspoken tomboy. As the story unfolds, because of the dramatic action, Scout is forced to control her temper and hold her tongue. At the same time, she slowly comes to appreciate that "there was some skill involved in being a girl."

Having come to a new understanding of herself and human nature in general, societal expectations, and her own place in the world throughout the story, by the story's end Scout is transformed into a young lady.

By tracking the character's development on the scene tracker under the character emotional development column, you are able to control what information is given and precisely in what order to make the most dramatic impact on the reader.

In much the same way, you can plot out the thematic significance of *To Kill a Mockingbird*. That no one really understands another person until she considers things from the other person's point of view is suggested several times in the first quarter of the book. When Scout is sent out of the dining room for inappropriate comments to her classmate, the reader "sees" her inability to stand in someone else's shoes.

Throughout the next half of the book, the theme is deepened and developed.

For instance, when Scout stands up to a mob of men who come to the jail for Tom Robinson, her actions force one man to see things from Atticus's point of view. After that, the man is unwilling to go through with the mob's original plan and talks his cohorts into dispersing.

Later in the middle, Scout asks herself why Boo stays shut inside his house. This reference deepens the thematic plot and represents the first time Scout consciously looks at things through someone else's eyes.

In the final quarter of the story, Scout shows that she has successfully integrated the thematic significance when she gives Boo a seat in the dark, knowing he will be more comfortable there. And later, after she escorts him home, standing on his porch, she sees the world as he has seen it throughout the years.

PLOT WHISPER

Stories that get the reader thinking resonate with meaning. Stories that open audiences up create opportunities for a shared experience with others. A promising story with a thematically rich climax leaves the reader to ponder the deeper meaning and, in that way, is sure to deliver success.

What is your story really saying? What do all the words you are writing add up to? Your story is a reflection of a truth—not necessarily true for all time, but true for the story itself and likely for you, too.

The protagonist has undergone a transformation. What does that mean?

Jot down in your journal the ideas that come to you.

New/Rediscovered or Uncovered Knowledge/Skills/ Understanding

Earlier in this book we discussed the importance of writing the first draft all the way through, because knowledge of the climax determines so many of the earlier decisions you need to make. The action the protagonist takes at the climax reveals what traits, knowledge, and skills are necessary for her to prevail. Thus, these necessary skills will be missing at the beginning and she will need to relearn or rediscover them throughout the middle. Some skills she will be learning for the first time, but the true skills necessary for success at the climax are rediscovered after having been lost or buried due to her backstory. This is a backward approach to developing a character, deconstructing the end character to determine who she is at the beginning.

We started this book with a forward approach to developing a character. You filled in a flaw, a strength, and five other character traits on the character profile. Either you begin writing first and the character reveals these traits to you, or you decide upon the character traits first and then construct a character using those traits. However, there are some writers who write from the climax back to the beginning.

In order for the character to transform, her traits also transform. If the protagonist needs patience in order to achieve her goal and face her greatest fear, in the beginning she is the antithesis of patient. Throughout the middle, her impatience trips her up more and more often, which causes her to react with frustration and anger.

THE WRITER'S WAY

In these last-quarter scenes, as the protagonist begins to develop and rely on her intuition, you do, too. You bring more discipline to your writing schedule. You trust yourself and the process of discovery. You keep your eye on your goal, knowing how near you are to success.

Then one day, the air goes out of you. You feel like a failure and find yourself falling all the way back to how you used to feel. You give up.

Rather than despair, celebrate. Throw yourself a party. Relax. Enjoy. You are already there.

Create a list of those parts of your old self most threatening to your new will. Each time you find yourself sinking into old patterns, grasp onto the wisdom you have learned about yourself as a writer. Your new insights are like life rafts to remind you of who you are becoming. They bring you strength.

Do whatever it takes to write, even if only for a few minutes. Each time you keep writing when you are convinced your story is a mess and you are unworthy, you are on your way to success.

Mastery does not mean that you will always be strong and confident, that you will always show up consistently to write and believe in yourself as a writer. Mastery means that you know yourself well enough now to use new strategies to pick yourself out of the muck more quickly and with fewer bruises.

I encountered an interesting illustration of the advantages of writing from the climax backward several years ago in a workshop I conducted. After ten years of writing and having completed barely the first quarter of her story, a writer, having worked through miles of resistance and pounds of fear, approached the end of her first draft and faced the climax. At this point in the story, she had to decide what she was truly writing about.

In each of her ideas of how to conclude the story, the character acted in ways that were clichéd and brought absolutely nothing new to the story. She wanted this book to be a "break-out" book for her, so she kept challenging herself to think outside the box.

Most books that break out express ideas that do not merely mirror the times. They unravel the time *and* transform it, evolving traditional thoughts into something new.

The writer struggled to identify what that new way might be, what it might look like, feel like, and sound like. She never had taken full responsibility for her own actions in her personal life, nor had she experienced a transformation in herself. Still, she didn't quit. Instead, she wrote backward from the climax and discovered along the way the real journey her character had been on. When she stepped back and looked at the finished product, she realized that the unique feature of her book had been there all along; she'd just been unable to see it.

Writing backward sounds counterintuitive, but it can be revolutionary.

The moment the protagonist takes the first step toward the completion of her final goal, she struggles to take full ownership of her newly discovered consciousness. The protagonist more and more painfully realizes each time her actions or speech do not align with her new understanding of herself and the world around her.

Even after rest and reflection at the threshold, the full integration of what is happening to her involves an adjustment period. She is cracked open. A blinding light floods into every part of her. She needs practice incorporating the depth and breadth of learning and connectedness into her being. She has not yet mastered her transformation. She may require one step forward, two steps back, and three forward on her way to the climax.

Demonstrating That New Self

At the climax, often the protagonist's greatest antagonist challenges her again. Unlike earlier encounters, however, this time, rather than be aggressive, the protagonist is assertive. Now she is able to turn the opposing energy into something helpful. Because of all the antagonists she has confronted in the story and learned from along the way, at the climax the character is able to show us yet another way to live life in triumph.

For many protagonists, especially those in character-driven stories, the character's backstory represents the loss of the imperfect imprint of her original self. In other words, something happens to the character that causes the protagonist to begin to doubt herself and to fear the world around her.

Because of all the dramatic action that takes place in the front story, by the climax the protagonist has uncovered and rediscovered her perfect imprint. In realigning herself to her inner purpose, for the first time since the backstory robbed her of herself, she meets herself as she truly is meant to be. She may fear what she faces at the climax, however, she no longer runs away from her fears. She confronts them head-on.

At the climax of *The Secret Life of Bees*, Lily's father shows up. Lily's transformation is revealed when, rather than being overcome with anger—her typical emotional reaction—she overcomes her anger. In this final life and death struggle, Lily wins by quiet and reason as she stands up to her greatest fear—her father—by refusing to leave where she is and return home with him.

Her fear in the dramatic action plot intensifies when Lily runs after her father and asks him the question whose answer she most fears: Did I fire the gun that killed my mother?

In action-driven stories, the greatest antagonist typically is represented as a universal external fear, such as a seemingly undefeatable villain or a force intent on destroying the world. At the climax, the protagonist confronts and defeats the greater antagonist for the good of the whole.

Internal, character-driven stories end more reflectively. Now, the protagonist stops making decisions based on what she "should do" according to an old belief system, society, or family and recreating situations that keep her stuck. She is no longer obedient and dependent, expecting and receiving punishments and rewards. She refuses to adhere to what she ought to do, how she should behave, and the expectations of other people. Instead, she follows her intuition, listens to herself, and opens herself to guidance.

She is determined to make a stand in her life and live her truth. Because that happens, the antagonists in her life intensify their resistance to her change and growth. The emotion of the story rises ever higher.

As she learns who respects her feelings, she makes better choices about how to spend her time and who to spend it with.

This shift in the protagonist threatens family members, coworkers, and friends. Her piece of the puzzle has changed; now the entire picture shifts and demands a readjustment of the total scheme. Unsettled, perplexed, irritable, anxious, and afraid of change for themselves, the people around her refuse to accept her change. Their refusal turns up the heat. Because that happens, the character has to stretch. Because she stretches, she makes mistakes and sometimes fails again.

The more mistakes the protagonist makes listening to her own heart and expressing her true emotions, the more she learns. Only now, she does not attach energy or emotion to her problems. Rather than reacting and creating more difficulty, she detaches. No longer dragging around a sack full of old issues, she is free and often finds herself almost floating.

Her earlier goal or outer purpose expands into something much larger now that she is empowered by consciousness. No longer desperate, her feelings of isolation, competition, and separation vanish. With a new sense of insight and appreciation of the greater mystery, she understands every act has consequences in the world at large. Her decision-making process becomes more certain and takes less time. She relies less on gathering and analyzing data and more on intuition and instinct.

The Awakening by Kate Chopin takes place in 1890s Louisiana within the upper class Creole society. Edna dreams of soaring above tradition, prejudice, and her responsibility to children intent on dragging her into the soul's savagery for the rest of her days. Between exposing the children to scandal or her death, the protagonist chooses death.

Her choice reflects her ultimate transformation. What begins as one woman's rebellion against her marriage and motherhood grows into an understanding of her true self. Taking command of her life, for the first time she willingly reins in her childlike desires to have her own way. Instead, she respects the wants and needs of her family and, at the same time, refuses to sacrifice the self she worked so hard to birth. Ultimately, she finds peace in the sea.

THE WRITER'S WAY

A writer living in the French Quarter of New Orleans attended a bookstore event featuring his favorite author, the same author who had been his inspiration to write a high-energy external action story that spurs an internal character emotional development transformational story. After the author talk, the writer waited in line for an autograph.

Rather than inspiring him—the attendee's own book was near completion and ready to submit—the event gave him pause. He has been so focused on finishing his story so he could submit it and become famous, he missed an important aspect of being a successful writer.

"The event made me realize if I don't enjoy the work, what's the point?" he said. "It has made me have a better time writing. I understand now that publication is not the prize. The work itself is."

You, too, have the choice to unplug from thoughts and beliefs that create limitations and drag you down. You can choose to plug into thoughts that create your future experiences, knowing you are at the right place in the right time and performing the right action.

CHAPTER TWELVE
DENOUEMENT: THE END AND A NEW BEGINNING

Every new beginning comes from some other beginning's end.

—Seneca

The climax is the peak, the highest energetic scene in the entire story. The story's pinnacle is the culmination of all the energy that came before the climax. At the climax, the protagonist shows mastery of her true self. Her actions relieve the pressure that has been building within the story and provide a cathartic release. Consequently, the energy of the story immediately drops as reflected on the final downward line of the plot planner for the resolution.

A story cannot continue for many pages after the goal is met at the climax. As soon as the story question is answered, the tension vanishes.

Resolving Plot Points

When the energy is spent, the story is over. This means you do not have much time to create a sense of balance and give closure to your story. Take the story further and, though most readers never want a story they love to end, even the most loyal reader loses enthusiasm.

By the very end of the story, the reader and the audience learn what happens to the protagonist now that most of the conflicts have been resolved. The resolution is sometimes called the denouement. Whatever name you give it, the final chapter shows the protagonist making peace with the past and returning to a right relationship with herself and the world around her.

The energy of the story drops after the climax because the primary story question of *transformation* is answered. However, deliberately leaving an unanswered question or two beyond the primary plot helps guarantee that the energy of the story lives on in the reader even after the last page.

Some genres dictate how a story resolves. According to the Romance Writers of America, a romance story always ends with a positive resolution of the primary love interest's relationship. In other women's fiction, the resolution of the romantic subplot can be a bit murkier.

A classic example of an unresolved ending is Margaret Mitchell's *Gone with the Wind*. A myriad of plots work together in this novel. The primary one that drives all others is the romantic tension between Scarlett O'Hara and Rhett Butler. Though it takes the death of her child, the climax of the story shows Scarlett's ultimate transformation when, finally, she opens her eyes to the truth about Ashley and turns away.

Because she is able to do that, she is able to declare her love for Rhett. But it's too late. He answers that his love is worn out. He leaves and the reader is left with the final question: Will they reunite or is their relationship severed forever? Cynics and realists maintain that Rhett is gone for good. His action in walking through the door into the mist symbolizes contraction of his character. He has been too badly hurt to respond when Scarlett, offering love for the first time in her life, expands her emotional horizons. Her character emotional development from the beginning of the story to the end might lead the reader to doubt she would just give up. Idealists believe Scarlett still has time to make things right with Rhett.

Leaving loose ends of subplots invites reader involvement and inter-action. A bond develops between the reader and the story, which often leads to loyal fans.

In the 1937 classic *Their Eyes Were Watching God* by Zora Neale Hurston, the protagonist, Janie, has a personal, internal goal that grows from her backstory and is formed in the absence of her mother. The story begins as Janie returns to town after a mysterious year-and-a-half absence. In Chapter Two, she begins a recollection of her life for a curious friend of hers, starting when she was young. By formatting the book as she does, Hurston begins and ends the book in real story time; however, the rest of the book is thrust back in time through an extended flashback. At the beginning of the story, Janie is defined by others, protected, and held apart. In the middle of the novel, one hus-band puts her to work in the fields and the next husband takes her as his possession. Each relationship challenge forces Janie to develop the inner strength she needs to reclaim that which has always been right-fully hers and thus, in the end, vanquish the power of her backstory.

By the time Janie's third husband dies, Janie has endured intense loneliness and constant ridicule, and she feels no sorrow about his death. The energy of the story quickens at the second energetic marker in the middle of the novel when Janie meets Mister Vergible Woods, better known as Tea Cake. With the arrival of Tea Cake, Janie recommits to her goal of finding and giving love. Tea Cake teaches her games and how to laugh again. He easily and unconditionally accepts her love and he loves her, too. His respect for her leads her for the very first time in the entire story to feel unconditionally accepted by the people important to her. No longer judged and defined by oth-ers, Janie discovers who she is and what she is capable of becoming through the power of love.

The story resolves after Tea Cake dies. Alone for the first time, Janie returns to Eatonville, the place she calls home, and the story cycles back to the same two people in the same setting as the beginning, with only an hour or two having elapsed. Her story of daring for her own inde-pendence in the face of harsh judgment inspires her dear friend. With

Tea Cake's love in her heart, Janie lives the personal freedom she has desired her entire life. Women's fiction of every imaginable plot carries similar themes of independence, responsibility, and courage.

In the two pages that follow the climax of *The Secret Life of Bees*, the story resolves and the book ends. The plot thread between Lily and her father is left open; the reader is never told whether or when the young girl will return home to her father.

Their Eyes Were Watching God was written in the 1930s about a woman who finds herself, through the convention of marriage, under the control of men. *The Secret Life of Bees*, set in the mid-1960s shortly before the women's movement, is the story of a girl who finds her voice in the safety of women.

The Awakening by Kate Chopin explores similar themes of finding and living fully within a woman's true self. In the final pages of the novel, the reader is not told whether Edna lives or dies. We do know she finds peace and thus resolves her character emotional plot. Rather than the story ending with images of death, a soothing childhood scene leaves the dramatic action plot unresolved. A question remains: Is she victorious for her independence and coming to know herself or, in the end, is she a victim by succumbing to convention and sacrificing herself for her children?

When someone real or imagined is transformed, the resolution is the writer's opportunity to tie together that thematic significance by showing the sum of the character's actions and making the story complete. However, as I've shown above, you can leave the end without a resolution so long as it is thematically true to the overall story.

The Transformed Protagonist Re-Enters the World

In the beginnings of stories, fear, competition, and the drive to succeed rule the protagonist's life.

By the middle, those same themes trick the protagonist into believing freedom is gained through the accumulation of material objects and money, publication, completion, recognition, accolades, and/or revenge.

PLOT WHISPER

Scan your life experiences. How do you handle endings? How did you leave your last relationship and the one before that? What about jobs or places in the past? In school, did you rush through assignments simply to be finished? Do you just want your book written and published already? At the end of vacation, do you luxuriate all the way up to the last minute, or do you turn your attention in anticipation of real life that awaits right around the corner? Often, we just let things peter out.

Writing the climax of your story is also the climax of your journey in creating a work of art. Before your writer's life story is over and it is time to celebrate, first determine how the resolution fits with the rest of the story.

- On a sticky note write a one-sentence title that represents the resolution of your story.
- What note color did you choose?
- Is what you wrote primarily thematic, character-driven, action-driven, or a combination of the three?
- Evaluate the linkage between the scenes that make up the final quarter of the book.
- Compare what happens in the first quarter of the book to what happens in the final quarter and what that means thematically overall to the story.

The crisis toward the end of the middle is the gateway to higher levels of awareness, where all mental, emotional, and physical distortions fall away.

The end of the story shows the building of a new personality and a sense of true freedom. The protagonist, now transformed, is able to rely on the use of her intuition for ultimate success at the climax.

At the resolution, the character is able to return to the world, and the story ends.

Often in the scene that resolves the story, the protagonist returns to the ordinary world of the beginning having survived the process of alchemy and transformed into something higher. In stories that circle back to the beginning, the protagonist places her new attributes in the service of her community—in Hurston's *Their Eyes Were Watching God*, Janie returns and her story inspires her friend. Her victory opens the possibility for a new world . . . but does not necessarily assure it.

Another example of a story that circles back to the beginning is the screenplay *Alice in Wonderland* by Linda Woolverton, adapted from Lewis Carroll's *Alice's Adventures in Wonderland* and *Through the Looking-Glass*. In the first scene of the screenplay, Alice's father relates a dream to a roomful of men. The final scene takes place twelve years later, when Alice returns to complete her father's work and fulfill that dream.

Character transformation in a story mirrors the Universal Story of rebirth. Rebirth contributes to the evolution of us all and delights those who harbor a secret belief in miracles. A character reunited with a long-lost part of herself speaks to the possibilities in our own lives. Our inner intelligence whispers of the timelessness of birth, growth, death, and renewal.

When a character undergoes a quest, the transformed character is left with a new status. She receives new privileges and responsibilities from her community. Her new attitude, beliefs, discoveries, and identity are gifts that strengthen, revitalize, and renew the past and the future members of the story world as well as the reader.

THE WRITER'S WAY

You managed to keep your head down and your spirits high throughout writing the first draft of your story. Sometimes the experience felt like an emotional rollercoaster ride, but you prevailed.

Congratulate yourself. You learned about yourself. You became a better writer. You successfully reached your goal. You can obsess about what comes next later. For now, close your eyes. Take a deep breath. You partnered with the muse and dedicated yourself to do your part to the best of your abilities. You wrote a novel, memoir, or screenplay from the beginning to the end. Feel it. Savor the good feelings. Be in the moment of your accomplishment.

Take time and good care of yourself. Sleep and eat well. Schedule long walks—perhaps to all the locations mentioned in your story. Wander and sleep; straighten up your writing area; purge and organize notes. Whatever you do, do not read your manuscript for at least a week to ten days.

As you give yourself time to shift from writing the first draft to preparing for the next one, view your writing life as unfolding in a series of experiences. Each has the three-phase form of separation/ordeal-learning/return. Each time you write again, you separate from your comfort zone, face ordeals, learn from them, and move forward.

For now, you are safely ensconced on the threshold between two worlds. Revel in the splendor of what you have done. Life will never be like this again.

CHAPTER THIRTEEN
SOME PARTING ADVICE

Fill your paper with the breathings of your heart.

—William Wordsworth

Each time you reach the end of your story, re-envision your story at the level of the Universal Story in preparation for a significant rewrite.

Revision Tips

Do not show your first draft to anyone. The first draft of a writing project is the generative phase. At the end of it, you are faced with a manuscript full of holes and missteps, even confusion and chaos. This is part of the process. Bringing in an unbridled critic risks stifling the muse and could intimidate you into stagnation.

Your first draft is a fragile thread of a dream. You know what you want to convey—well, maybe. Few writers adequately communicate a complete vision in the first draft of a story, especially when writing by the seat of your pants. Allow others to read your writing now and you may lose energy for your story and become overwhelmed by the task ahead of you.

Do not read what you have written. The longer you give yourself before actually reading your first draft, the better. Distance allows you to read your work more objectively later.

Fill out the character emotional profile for the protagonist as she is at the end of the story. Do not refer to the first profile you created until after you have filled it out again. Now, with the entire story in mind, compare the two profiles—before and after. Analyze how the protagonist shows herself transformed. Determine what is missing and evaluate what's been added. How do her goals and traits change?

Refer to your plot planner and make a list of scenes in order from beginning to end.

Track each scene or, at least, track the energetic markers and any other major turning points. This shows you which plot elements are missing and which are in the scene in its current condition.

Seven Plotting Questions

For each scene, ask yourself the seven essential questions of plot:

1. Does the scene establish the date and setting?
2. How does it develop the character's emotional makeup?
3. Is the scene driven by a specific character goal?
4. What dramatic action is shown?
5. How much conflict, tension, suspense, or curiosity is shown?
6. Does the character show emotional changes and reactions within the scene?
7. Does the scene reveal thematic significance to the overall story?

For the scenes that are less strong in advancing the story through all the elements of plot, consider how you can integrate more plot elements. You may be able to combine two or more weak scenes to make one powerful scene.

Detach from the time, thought, and emotion that went into writing these scenes. If the scene does not carry enough weight to qualify for inclusion, cut it. Be ruthless.

Evaluate the scene tracker for your strengths and weaknesses as a writer. If you find your scene tracker has lots of dramatic action filled with conflict, tension, and suspense, but little character emotional development, plan in your rewrite to concentrate on developing your weakness.

Using the same list of scenes you created for the scene tracker exercise, make a new plot planner for your story. Locate and fill in the four energetic markers—the end of the beginning, the halfway point, the crisis, and the climax.

1. Assign different colored sticky notes for the protagonist and one or two major characters. Give all the other characters the same color. Link the protagonist's emotional chronology from scene to scene.
2. Sticky notes of one color follow the energetic intensity in the dramatic action in every scene, above or below the line. Place scenes that hold tension above the line. Put scenes with no conflict below the line. Evaluate how many scenes fall above and below the line, and where. Consider how the rising and falling energy influences the pace of the story.
3. Compare the beginning and the end of your story. How do they tie together? Do both the dramatic action plot and character emotional development plot coalesce at the end for more punch and impact? Does the beginning foreshadow this clash?
4. Draw a line connecting the scenes that are linked by cause and effect. To determine the coherence of the overall story and the linkage between scenes, use your plot planners as a cause-and-effect vision board.

- Focus on the first scene on the plot planner. See the characters and actions in your mind's eye.
- Watch your protagonist move from the first scene to the next scene in the story.
- As if watching a film, let each scene play out moment-by-moment to the end of the story. Instead of seeing the words of the story on the computer screen, see the action take place with the help of the plot planner.

- Look for openings for each scene to foreshadow an upcoming energetic marker and major turning point in the character emotional development plot and in the dramatic action plot.
- As you "see" the story unfold in your mind's eye, note any person or place that symbolizes a cauldron. A hot spot that periodically arises in the story and shakes up the character becomes a thematic causal-echo and helps to tie the story together.
- How well does the story flow from the cause to the effect?

You invite the reader into the imaginary world of your story. The tighter the causality, the easier it is for the reader to follow and thus surrender to the dream the story creates.

Arranging Scenes by Cause and Effect

Every element of every scene contributes to the scene that follows and to the overall story itself. The elements that vary are the beat or tempo and the intensity.

Compare, for example, the bestseller *The DaVinci Code*, a dramatic action-driven story by Dan Brown, to the more leisurely plot pace of the early nineteenth-century novel *Emma* by Jane Austen, a character emotional development-driven story. Though the degree of intensity rises at differing speeds, both stories possess strong elements of suspense, thanks to the use of tightly linked cause and effect.

Today, writers have widened tremendously the way they can tell stories. But whether you adhere to the current storytelling standards or create your own, and whether you write thrillers, memoirs, historical, or mainstream fiction, a firm understanding of cause and effect increases your chances of being published and enjoyed by readers.

If you find yourself moving from scene to scene, merely reciting what happens in each scene and finding little linkage between them, you have not yet mastered the art of deliberately arranging a series of events by cause and effect.

Without cause and effect there is no plot. Without a sense of unity and causality, scenes are simply episodic occurrences. The tempo and intensity of a story becomes strident and discordant, chopped into bits and pieces.

In this area, writers who write by the seats of their pants have the advantage over writers who pre-plot before and during writing, because "pantsers" often craft entire stories through cause and effect.

Kathleen Duey, an author of more than fifty books for children, middle graders, and young adults, is a classic right-brained, big-picture, highly creative pantser. She and *New York Times* bestselling romance novelist Brenda Novak, and others like them, write entire novels scene by scene, asking: *because this happens in this scene, what does the character do next?*

1. Random incidents don't move us, nor do they illuminate or provide meaning. We want to know why one thing leads to another. Your readers expect the events that unfold in a scene to have repercussions.
2. Locate preparatory scenes. To what degree do they set up feelings of anticipation in the audience?
3. Which scenes foreshadow upcoming major turning points and energetic markers in the character emotional development plot and the dramatic action plot?

A good story seduces a reader by the illusion it creates. As the reader sinks into the world of the characters on the page, she surrenders her emotions to the illusion. This strengthens as the reader comes to know the characters and care for them, even worry about them. The reader's body responds on a visceral level; her heart beats faster. Perhaps she laughs or weeps, so involved is she in the story world.

Creative Foreshadowing

Foreshadowing is a literary device that alludes to something that will happen later in the story. It is subtle way to draw the reader deeper into the illusion with the promise of excitement to come. In the beginning, or the first quarter of the page count or scene count, foreshadows actually appear as introductions.

Harper Lee in *To Kill a Mockingbird* uses foreshadowing to strengthen the illusion of the story world. At the beginning of the story, while in the mode of narrator of the story, Scout tells the reader, "Inside the (neighboring) house lived a malevolent phantom." Later, her brother elaborates on that description to their new friend Dill:

> Boo was about six-and-a-half feet tall, judging from his tracks; he dined on raw squirrels and any cats he could catch, that's why his hands were blood-stained—if you ate an animal raw, you could never wash the blood off. There was a long jagged scar that ran across his face; what teeth he had were yellow and rotten; his eyes popped, and he drooled most of the time.

At the first energetic marker we learn that Scout was "so busy looking at the fire you didn't know it when [Boo] put the blanket around you." The reader now has a sense that Boo is not what he first appeared. This act of Boo's foreshadows the climax of the story. The reader's curiosity about who Boo really is draws her into the heart of the story.

Lee also introduces Burris Ewell in the beginning through the medium of his son, a classmate of Scout's. Burris is filthy, a down-hard mean man liable to start something. Because Lee introduces the boy and mentions his father, we are not surprised when we learn in the middle of the story what the father has done.

Much later in the story, in the middle of the end, after Tom Robinson commits suicide, we learn that Burris has threatened to kill two more men.

Soon after that the judge, who embarrassed Burris in the trial, discovers an attempted break-in at his house. If the reader had not already figured it out, she now knows for sure one of the people Burris was alluding to. The reader becomes afraid for Atticus—clearly the third man—and turns the pages faster. When Aunt Alexandra stops short in the middle of her sentence as somebody walks over her grave, the reader feels the sensation as well.

Even as the reader sees Scout in her Halloween costume and is caught up in the light-hearted fun of her presentation to the family and Calpurnia, the stiff hairs on the back of the reader's neck do not relax. When Jem escorts Scout to the pageant and their friend pops out behind the big oak tree to frighten them, the sense of doom heightens. On the way home after the pageant, when Jem and Scout approach that same tree, the reader knows the climax is near.

The best reading occurs when the reader is so under the trance of the story that he does not want to put the book down. Foreshadowing helps create this feeling in the reader. He cannot stop until he finds out if what he thinks will happen (based on clever foreshadowing) *does*, in fact, occur.

The visual representation of your project on a plot planner gives you clues as to where to interject foreshadowing in the rewrite.

PLOT WHISPER

Mark the flashbacks on your list. How far does the flashback(s) take the reader out of the here-and-now of the story world? Is the flashback worth reminding the reader the story is only an illusion and risk weakening the trance you created, even break it?

Using your list of scenes, write a brief outline of your story by chapter—simply one or two sentences per chapter. This gives you a feel for pacing, plot, and flow. The process of writing the outline often reveals holes and weaknesses in the story.

Synopsize

Write a one-page synopsis of your story. Writing a synopsis can be as demanding as writing the entire book. A synopsis distills the story to its essence. Search for an underlying thematic thread. Consider who is your reader. This helps you get a sense of what to concentrate on in the next draft.

Read the back and inside flap covers of the jackets of ten books you admire or that are similar in style or tone to the book you are writing. Write a jacket blurb for your book without giving away the plot. This exercise helps you visualize the final work as a book.

Revisit the theme bubbles you created early in the process of writing your story. Cross out all but the strongest themes. Consider the thematic significance statement in the main bubble in light of all you now know about the bigger picture of your story. Keep tweaking the thematic statement by using different combinations of the theme words from the smaller bubbles.

THE WRITER'S WAY

Often, when fulfilling the above suggestions, calamity hits. Coffee spills on the manuscript or the scene tracker rips. Perhaps, you stub your toe, break the pencil lead, or yell at the dog for tracking muddy paws across your plot planner. If this happens, note the resistance.

Accidents are a rebellion against authority. Ask yourself: To whom or what am I giving up my authority? Perhaps you have given your power over to the belief that this stuff is too hard or that you have always hated organization and plotting. As much as you like the generative stage, you hate the revision and rewriting stages. Who is ever going to want to read your work anyway? You are not smart enough to get this. Your story is no good. Your story is so great you do not need all this added work. Could be, you are racing to complete the assignment because so many other things demand your attention.

You have the choice to buck up and do the work or be mired in the muck. I vote that you get back into your body and reclaim your power. The work you are doing is important. It deserves the time you take to get this right.

At the beginning of this book I told you to simply start writing, using whatever words came to you. Now you know the characters better than you did initially, and you have a sense of the themes and significance of your story. Decide the story's ideal starting place, what many writers call the inciting incident. Stand back from all the words you have written and ask yourself how you can best begin showing the protagonist now doing what creates the most contrast to what she does at the end.

A scene that shows the protagonist taking action in a thematically true and characterized way is a good place to start.

Read Your Manuscript

After letting your story (and you) rest, read your manuscript all the way through one time as a reader. Keep the next draft in the back of your mind. You may find you have completely zoned out about the character's emotions in your zeal to create lots of zip and zing in the dramatic action, or in your passion to create a binding historical and/or political timeline. Notice when the dramatic action plot is physical and concrete. Feel when the character emotional plot is emotional, sensuous, and human. Read for the sequence of the dramatic action and where, in the next draft, you'll want to explore and discover the character's emotional development in greater depth.

If, when you reread your manuscript, you find that you have neglected the dramatic action plot, create concrete goals in the next draft that incite the protagonist to action.

Investigate how the loss, betrayal, hurt, or abandonment in the protagonist's backstory affects her as she moves from and reacts to one action scene after another. Watch for references and hints of themes, and when and how thematic elements of the plot are most accessible.

In the next read-through, make notes on the rough draft hard copy of scenes that need to be cleaned up, expanded, and deepened in their treatment of the characters, action, and theme.

You may find the first draft is wobbly and scenes ramble. The complete vision of your story was a bit hazy the first time through. The action was tangled. The protagonist comes off as bewildering. You have glossed over an energetic marker or two. Don't panic—this is good. As a matter of fact, the worse the first draft, the better. Trying for perfection before you know what you are trying to convey commonly leads to procrastination, as we discussed in Chapter One.

Changing your expectations and giving yourself permission to be sloppy the first time around is difficult for many writers and seemingly impossible for self-professed perfectionists. But if you can do it, it will ease the pressure and increase the joy of discovery in your writing.

Rewriting Tips

Do not be surprised if you feel ready to begin rewriting, eager even to start with the inciting incident you conjured up, and instead you clean your house, get a new job, begin a new project, or do anything besides write. Months go by. Rather than recommit to your story and embark on writing the next draft, you read every book on the craft of writing. You fill out countless character studies and labor over forms and graphs.

By constantly analyzing scenes, you keep your emotions at bay. You search for just the right trick for creating a compelling plot. The more you delay, the more your emotions begin to crack.

Rather than think your story out, write and feel it. Rather than look at all the time and dedication it took to write the first draft of your story, commit to giving up even more time and effort for the next draft.

Start writing the next draft in your strength or preference as you set your protagonist off in pursuit of a tangible goal(s). In other words, if you have found from the exercises you have done throughout this book that you seem to favor more left-brained aspects of writing, such as creating dramatic action scenes with high tension and suspense, start there. If, on the other hand, you have found your preference is exploring the characters and the impact their emotions have on their behavior, start there.

As you rewrite, follow the notes you made on the hard copy. Refer to the scene tracker and plot planner. Once you catch your rhythm, try writing from your weakness. In other words, confront your flaws—and those of your characters—head-on. Reveal the protagonist's emotional reactions as she confronts antagonists on her way to wholeness.

THE WRITER'S WAY

Writers at the end of a plot workshop often share revelations about their writing. One writer announced that when he arrived, his story was all history and philosophy. Now he understood that the character emotional development comes first and the other elements belong in the background. The reader has to relate to and care about the protagonist before she cares about the history and philosophy. Realizing this energized this writer to dig back into a story he had let languish for years.

Another writer said that though his new understanding was obvious to him now, he finally "got it" that people read to see what happens to the character emotionally, that the character emotional development is what drives the story. He went on to say that nothing is more infuriating than spilling your deepest emotions and truth about yourself to a blank wall, getting no emotional reaction. He was determined to not hold back in the next draft, and finished by saying that what we all want is to know we have been heard.

These two writers, and others like them, benefited in the second draft by slowing down and concentrating on character. Rather than imagine what they would do in the scenes they were setting up, they asked what the character would do—an important difference.

After reading this book, what revelations are you taking with you about your writing, your story, your life, and yourself?

As you did with the first draft, write this new draft as quickly as possible all the way to the end. Work out the really big issues first and forget about the details for now. As you write, trust that what is yours is unique and perfect, whole and complete.

When you finish the next draft and you are certain that the core dramatic action plot and character emotional development plot work, use the next rewrite to begin grafting on details.

CHAPTER FOURTEEN
SOME FINAL THOUGHTS

Easy reading is damn hard writing.

—Nathaniel Hawthorne

At the beginning of this book you were promised transformation. Pull out the writer's profile you filled in for yourself in Chapter Five. Review your answers.

- How have your goal and your flaw shifted while reading this book and writing your story?
- Where are you along the way to successfully accomplishing your writing goal?
- Of the real or imagined internal and external obstacles, which one(s) continue to block your success?
- While plotting and writing your story, what strengths have you found that you never imagined for yourself?
- What have you lost along the way?
- What have you gained?
- Who are you as a writer, and as a person today?

Using the Scene Tracker

To reduce such an illusion as a story to the scrutiny of a linear, boxed-in, organized system is not very romantic. Yet using the scene tracker strengthens and builds a story's vital essence and clears a path for writing dynamic scenes. What separates a truly great writer from a merely good one is the ability to assess what writing stays in the story and, more important, what does not. The scene tracker brings finesse to scenes by evaluating each scene's strengths and weaknesses.

The plot planner allows you to plot at the overall story level. The scene tracker shows essential plot elements at the scene level. In both cases, you can stand back from the words and view the entire story as a whole and see the Universal Story beneath the story.

In analyzing novels, memoirs, and screenplays, I have determined that at least seven elements appear in most scenes. These seven essential elements, mentioned earlier, are:

1. Where and when the scene takes place
2. Character emotional development
3. Character short-term goal
4. Action taken toward that goal
5. Conflict, tension, suspense, and/or curiosity
6. Emotional fluctuations within each scene
7. Thematically rich authentic details.

The scene tracker enables you to examine each scene in your story to determine whether the scene is working hard enough to deserve staying. The scene tracker also gives clues on how to expand weak scenes and make all your scenes truly great.

Release the Energy

At the close of every healing session, I shake the energy off my hands and, when possible, wash my hands with soap and water. I do this as a symbolic gesture, releasing the energy from the work I just preformed and, as a ritual, to invite in the energy of what comes next.

With every story there comes a time to give thanks for the work by letting it go. You are the steward of the story. It never was yours to begin with. The manuscript represents a work that transformed you.

Write down your vision for what comes next for the final draft of your story as a long-term goal. Divide that goal into short-term goals that represent steps you believe will best achieve your long-term book goals.

Releasing your story may take one or more forms:

- Allow those who ask to read it.
- Submit your work to a literary contest.
- Query an agent.

Pick one or all of the above and send your story out into the world to face its own set of challenges. Submitting your work for others to evaluate and judge is never easy, but then writing it in the first place was not easy either. Before making a copy of the story or filling in the contest entry form or dashing off your first query letter, release old beliefs that do not fit you anymore. You already have purged scenes and chapters that lacked a thematic thread leading to the climax. Just as the release of those unnecessary words frees your story to embrace a new identity, you are free to create a higher and more vibrant meaning to your life.

Release Your Ego When You Release Your Book

You have three choices about how to react to feedback from others:

1. Your body shrinks and withdraws. Negative words crowd your mind. You give up.
2. You become angry and belligerent, reject constructive criticism that could be helpful.
3. You consider the feedback and intent thematically. You wake up and move ahead.

You know now that you are more than the words you write and the books you publish. You are a writer. Because you are a writer, you listen differently to other people's judgments about your words and your books.

Having interacted with thousands of writers, I find universally that they exhibit deep emotion when writing a story. The better able you are to face that emotion, the better able you are to use it to your advantage.

Adapt the exercise you did for your story themes in Chapter Four to determine the level of resistance and emotion you feel as a writer. Draw a bubble in the middle of a piece of paper. Write your deepest held beliefs about yourself, the ones that prevent you from having what you want most.

- I am not good enough.
- I am not smart enough.
- Tending to my ailing mother, my dying father, my young child is more important than my writing.
- I do not deserve the kind of time it takes to write a screenplay.

Pick one. Create one. We all have them.

Spiraling out from the bubble, create other bubbles, each with an external antagonist who has the potential to send you off track: accidents, bad men, addictions, drama, dead-end jobs, illnesses, half-finished projects, arguments, conflict, conflict, conflict, blockage, blockage, blockage . . . .

Who and what (antagonists) have you gone up against lately? Who or what stands in the way of your happiness? Friends and family? Societal norms, handicaps, or you yourself?

Which of your fears, prejudices, and flaws continue to prevent you from achieving what you long for? How do you sabotage yourself?

The Stories We Tell

We make up stories in our minds about events in our lives. Are the stories real? Real only to us and only as far as our perception is capable of seeing at the time. The stories we tell ourselves to make sense of the world around us have a direct impact on how we react to new events. That's why one writer is slain by the antagonists that pop up along her writing journey, whereas another writer faced with the same problems is able to make her way forward.

Replace the story you tell yourself about writing from one of threat and opposition to one of strength and determination. Antagonists are self-created and have authority over you only so long as you surrender your own power.

You dream of writing the Great American Novel, but not because of the status or money it will bring. Having surrendered the pursuit of greatness, you stay in the now, writing one word in one scene on one page at a time, creating prose that works for the greatest good of the story.

You face every major threshold of your life now with the knowledge that fear is based on a fantasy of a danger that has not happened. You detach from the outcome and concentrate on putting words on the page. You forget the duality of good versus bad. You marvel and give thanks for the miracle of words appearing out of nowhere for you to write down.

You replace fear with blind trust that you are supported and that all is well. You make the act of writing, and everything you do, an act of love.

Moving On

A finished story held in your hands represents the achievement of one long-term goal and the climax in your writing journey, so far.

Invite in the energy of the next project. Put your trusty journal on your nightstand. In the twilight between wakefulness and sleep, ask for visions and dreams that represent a new story. Be prepared to embark on an entirely different journey with its own characters, action, themes, and energetic markers to approach and conquer along the way.

GET BUSY WRITING

A writer writes. Sure, she also plots and analyzes and reads books, but mostly a writer writes. When the energy goes out of you for your story, and plotting, analyzing, and reading books does nothing to pump you back up about that story, start a new one. Follow the energy and you will never go wrong. (Unless, of course, your core wound revolves around never completing anything. In that case, feel the emotion as you push forward to the end at least one time and in any way you can.)

You have written to where you are. Consider where you would like to be. What must you shed to get there? What must you learn? As you move toward your ideal, you carry with you all you have learned.

WRITER'S PROFILE

Fill in the writer's profile for yourself again as a writer and then compare it to the first one you filled out. Things look different and reflect all you have learned about yourself. When you write a new story, you never come back to the place you started from because each time the energy cycles, you take with you what you have learned.

The pace of the Universal Story moves to the rhythm of being and presence. What you do today is simply catching up to what already is.

Learning comes like drafts, one layer, one workshop, one book at a time. Take what works for you in this book and make it your own.

Get Along or Go Ahead?

You can fight what comes into your life or coast through it unconsciously. Or, if you buy into the idea of a Universal Story, you can direct its course. Such a belief comes down to one thing: What do you want? If your goal is to finish your story, what is stopping you?

I do not pretend that any of this is easy. Two steps forward, one step back. As long as you actively pursue your dream, your life expands. In that expansion, you consciously align your actions with your true self and forward movement seems effortless.

One of Many

This book is likely one of many on your writing shelf. If you write fantasy, paranormal, or science fiction, you have references that point out the special considerations beyond plot and the Universal Story for your genre. Books written specifically for authors writing Regency romance novels tell you where to place the first kiss. The Universal Story offers clues into when to expose the first dead body in a murder mystery, but the details of the genre require specialized treatment. Writing a screenplay demands special rules such as only things that can be seen and heard are included in the action. A memoir, because you are the protagonist, allows for more narrative and less dialogue than a blockbuster summer read.

Never stop searching for clues, for pointers, for company, and support. The more you research the craft of writing and the more you write, the better prepared you are to deal with the challenges that arise along the way.

Read award-winning novels, memoirs, or screenplays in your genre in order to learn more about plot and the Universal Story.

Analyze these works, using the tools you've encountered here. Study reference books with tips and advice from great authors and teachers of the genre. Attend writing conferences. Take classes. Link up with a critique group. Join a writing club. Visit your local bookstore. Become a member of a book group.

My wish is that every time you find yourself pushing against the boundaries of your comfort zone and into the great unknown of a story world, you pull this book off the shelf. Read it to remind yourself why you should go to the trouble of birthing a new story, why you should suffer that angst and those challenges, and grow and change and live a more expanded, joyful life.

Every story ever told includes something happening (dramatic action plot) to someone (character emotional development plot) in a meaningful way (thematic significance plot).

Because you have read this book and written a story, you are different. You can step back from your plot planner and measure your entire life against the Universal Story.

Perhaps there, you spot flickering in the smoldering ashes a glimpse of who you used to be. A backstory spell breaks. You are freed.

Each time you return to this book you are reminded of the transformation you have undergone and the promise of what awaits you.

INDEX